James P Taylor

How a Schoolmaster Became a Catholic

James P Taylor

How a Schoolmaster Became a Catholic

ISBN/EAN: 9783337395544

Printed in Europe, USA, Canada, Australia, Japan

Cover: Foto ©Lupo / pixelio.de

More available books at **www.hansebooks.com**

HOW A SCHOOLMASTER BECAME A CATHOLIC:

BY

JAMES P. TAYLOR.

Non est pudor ad meliora transire.—St. Ambrose.

REVISED EDITION.

LINDSAY, ONT.
THE CANADIAN POST BOOK DEPARTMENT
1890.

DIOCESE OF PETERBOROUGH. BISHOP'S HOUSE, PETERBOROUGH, ONT. July 30th, 1889.

The work entitled, "How a Schoolmaster became a Catholic," is the production of a thoughtful and studious enquirer, who was determined to be a real Protestant, in the sense of one who is not afraid to exercise his private judgment, by examining things to get at the truth and decide for himself. The author had sufficient confidence in the champions of Protestantism to believe that, in fair controversy, they could defend it against all assaults from Catholics, and drive all their enemies from the field. He gives the result of his reading and examination of the many charges against the Catholic Church, by ample quotations from both Protestant and Catholic writers of Church History and Controversial Works. We recommend this book to all who desire to know the truth, as it will enlighten them on many points that are falsely charged against the Church, and will show the true character of many of her assailants. A work like this deserves to be widely circulated and carefully read by both Catholics and Protestants, who sincerely seek to find out the reality and truth of the facts of Church History, as well as the source of most of the calumnies disseminated against the Church of Christ.

† R. A. O'CONNOR,
Bishop of Peterborough.

Approved also by His Lordship † Bishop RYAN of Buffalo And by His Grace † Archbishop RYAN of Philadelphia, Who says, "The book has solid merit."

"You have succeeded in grouping together in a very small space the principal proofs of Catholic principles, and in answering the objections commonly made to those principles in a satisfactory, and in many instances, original manner. Your book is an armory in which the Catholic can always find sufficient ammunition for defence and attack as well. It should have a large circulation as it is instructive to the Catholic and non-Catholic alike."—Rev. Father Lambert, Author of "Notes on Ingersoll," etc.

PRESS NOTICES.

Mr Taylor's reasoning is very good, and throughout his book he exhibits much humor which makes the work very pleasant reading. It is especially rich in very valuable and cogent extracts from Protestant authorities, proving that the common objections against the Catholic faith are founded on misconception or misrepresentation, and the extracts have been carefully taken directly from the works quoted. It is an excellent book to lend or present to Protestants who wish to know something tangible and easy of access respecting the [...] religion.—*Catholic Record*, London, Ont.

Told by himself as the story is, there is an absence of egotis[m in] its pages which cannot be too highly commended, and a careful thoroughness of treatment of all questions which one would not have expected to find in an unpretentious volume like the book before us. . . . We congratulate him on reaching the true haven of rest, and hope that the record of his experiences may guide many of his fellow mariners into the same port.—*Ave Maria*, Indiana.

"How a Schoolmaster Became a Catholic" is the modest title of a valuable controversial work. The book is well written and full of sound instruction for the seeker after truth in religion, while its plain binding and cheapness add to its recommendation for general circulation.—*Angelus*, Detroit.

Though professedly a desultory work, it is a useful contribution to controversial literature, and contains a large amount of valuable testimony in favor of the Catholic Church.—*Standard*, Philadelphia.

This is a most interesting and instructive work from the pen of Jas. P. Taylor of Lindsay. The writer is a convert. . . The book consists of a series of letters written in a versatile and entertaining style. Abundant proofs are given from Holy Scripture, reason, tradition, and the Fathers, that the Catholic Church is, and can be, the only true Church.—*Freeman's Journal*, New York.

We especially recommend its perusal to our Protestant friends whom we know to be sincere, but in error, as was ourself at one time.—*Western Catholic News*, Chicago.

The writer treats of the historical and, in a limited way and in so far as a layman can, of the doctrinal sides of the question, and does so, it must be said, in a very simple and intelligible and convincing manner. The main subjects treated are those objections against the Catholic Church, which are oftenest upon the lips of our Protestant brethren—the questions, for example, of religious persecution, the Church and learning, the temporal power of the Popes, Monasticism, and so forth, and the manner of treatment tends to show how calculated an intelligent course of reading is to dispel summarily, and once for all, the vulgar and current misconceptions in which, in the majority of non-Catholic minds, these questions are enveloped. The author has read a good deal of Church history, and quotes effectively from a considerable number of Protestant and Catholic writers. In fact, we are unable to conceal from ourselves, that he has furnished what may prove to be a useful little book to put in the hands of such of his former brethren as remain in heresy; and this somewhat negative approval will perhaps prove more acceptable if we say that on taking up the book all our predispositions were against it . . . We shall be glad to hear that the work has had a large circulation.—*Catholic Review*, Toronto.

Mr. Taylor's book is curious and unique, so much so that book buyers will miss an occasion if they fail to supply themselves with this odd volume. . . It is an acute discussion of those objections which every-day uninstructed Protestants bring against the Catholic Church. The book, . . is the most curious book we have ever seen.—*Catholic Review*, New York.

NOTICE.

The following letters, which first appeared in the "Catholic Record," I have been persuaded, after having made several though immaterial alterations, to offer in book shape; and the persuasion of friends is the only apology I make for re-presenting them. Written at snatch chances, they carry all the marks of desultory work; but I have taken the greatest care in testing the accuracy of the quotations, which, unless specially indicated, are taken directly from the works named.

Lindsay, Xmas., 1888.   J. P. T.

CONTENTS.

LETTER.		PAGE.
I.	INTRODUCTION	9
II.	PERSECUTION	16
III.	THE CHURCH AND LEARNING	27
IV.	MONASTICISM	36
V.	FRAGMENTS	48
VI.	TEMPORAL POWER OF THE POPES	68
VII.	'REFORMERS' AND 'REFORMATION.'	81
VIII.	REVIEW AND ADVANCE	100
IX.	THE CHURCH	107
X.	THE CHURCH (CONTINUED)	118
XI.	RULE OF FAITH	130
XII.	PRIMACY OF ST. PETER	138
XIII.	ANGLICANISM	160
XIV.	TRANSUBSTANTIATION	183
XV.	A MISCELLANY	197

LETTER I.

INTRODUCTION.

When a man abjures Protestantism and embraces the Catholic faith, his gross misconduct becomes the subject of serious and varied speculation. He has entered into the first stages of lunacy; or a low craving for notoriety has had the better of him; or it may have been an act of perverse folly, to gratify some personal spite; or the expectation of some temporal advantage explains it all. What excuse can he offer for himself? Freedom of conscience was his birthright; in the pure precepts of the Gospel he had been, or might have been, carefully nurtured; and with the superstitions, corruptions, and immoralities of the Catholics he must have been perfectly familiar: but he has wilfully submitted to the tyranny of a corrupt and designing priesthood, and in all human probability has imperilled the salvation of his soul. Before the world he stands a wretched apostate from the faith of his fathers. He cannot make a reasonable or honest defence of his conduct. Perhaps not; but it is precisely what I purpose to attempt.

And at the outset I will observe, that, as a good disposition of material strengthens a position, I should try to throw what I have to say into the form of a coherent whole; but, were I to do so, I should not retrace the successive steps that led me into the Church. I did not study Catholicity in a regular way. When I first meddled with Catholic books, I did so more from a chance curiosity than from any intention of soberly examining the claims of the Church upon my belief. Had I been challenged to survey and seriously consider those claims, receiving at the same time the slightest intimation, that my faith in Protestantism might thereby be shaken, I should have treated the challenge with becoming scorn. In that case I should never, perhaps, have been a son of the Church.

Cornwall, the "County of Saints," is my native county. What Cornishman, exiled for years, will not experience a thrill of rapture on hearing pronounced the names of St. Ewe, St. Neot, St. Cleather, St. Blazey, St. Ives, and innumerable other Catholic Saints, which are stamped on the parishes of lovely Cornwall. And it was in this county, formerly bedewed with the tears of Saints, consecrated by their labors, and still containing precious monuments of their religion, that I was taught to believe in John Wesley! Very early I was instructed in his catechism, and jealously confined to Methodistic influences. My parents, both ardent Methodists, piously believed, that they were instilling into my mind the pure truths of Christianity; and to their zealous endeavors I am indebted for a belief in Christianity that I have never been able to stifle. They did for me what they believed the best; if I have partly disappointed their hopes, I can not help it. Before God I believe I am right: I am certain of it. I joined the Catholic Church to please nobody, nor to displease anybody.

The first time, in my recollection, that I heard any thing of the Catholics was in 1851, when Cardinal Wiseman was appointed Archbishop of Westminster. Then there was a great stir in the parish. The parson scandalized the neighborhood by putting a small cross on his church. To propitiate the Catholics, a distant but terrible enemy, he was relapsing into idolatry. So much was apparent to the native sense of every one, and was seasonably confirmed and dilated upon by the gentleman that filled the Methodist pulpit. John Wesley's profile, which was cut in granite, by a local artist, and which surmounted the portal of the Methodist chapel in Alternun, was something of too holy an aspect for the lowest accent of censure; but the cross on the church had a bad look! Cardinal Wiseman's advent excited the gravest fears. Would he gain the upper hand, and start the stake-and-faggot business? The general opinion was, that, unless he received a timely check, there would soon be a general conflagration of preachers, class-leaders, and their supporters.

This was the first time that I heard the Catholics freely discussed, and what could a boy do but believe what nobody disputed. It was worked into me very early, then, that the Catholics are a treacherous, blood-thirsty crowd of ignorant idolaters. Several readings of Fox's Martyrs little modified my first impressions, and every book that I read gave the same black account of them.

In 1857, I was removed to Canada, and in the same year I entered a printing-office to learn the trade. I soon mastered "the case," and, after a trial of six months, the proprietor wished me to be indentured. But it had been found out that he was a Catholic. The danger was great. The class-leader was very properly consulted: the decision was, that "the boy might be lost." The boy was taken to the woods, to learn the handicraft of bush-whacking. It was a hard life. All day long throughout the winters I chopped; but during the long nights I read every book I could come across in the settlement. The only mental excitement in the place to be enjoyed, was the annual, protracted meeting in the E. M. C. Every year the same batch "got converted:" every year they went through the same antics and gave out the same groans, declaring all the while that their happiness was something indescribable ; and every year each and every one asserted, that "this conversion is," to use their particular expression, "genuine." I ridicule no one. I am putting things as they actually happened. But what puzzled me was, that "the Spirit" should force these people into such capers and never excite the Methodist congregation in the town of Whitby. I was only a boy though, and it was not for me to judge of such things.

The black-coated dignitaries that declaimed from the pulpit of that "meeting-house" posed as the infallible expounders of the Gospel and the true exponents of orthodoxy. Their knowledge of other denominations, too, was profound and exact, and their statements quite decided. The Anglicans were too Romanish to be recognized ; the Baptists of all shades held opinions that had no Scriptural warrant ; while the Presbyterians with their stern Predestinarianism sadly needed light. Of course, they thoroughly understood the craftiness and the falseness of the Catholic Church, and had a pious abhorrence of her pretensions. While I sat at the feet of these men, I heard the most extravagant laudations of Protestantism. It was every thing good,—tolerant, humane, the diffuser of light, the assertor of man's rights, the sole dispenser of God's Holy Word, and the sure director of man to heaven. But all this was simply emphasizing what I already knew. For years not a sign of distrust disturbed me about my Protestantism. I was as sound a Protestant as a Belfast Orangeman ; and, as far as a knowledge of Christianity is concerned, just about as ignorant. But I was to be a more intelligent Protestant.

A few years after I began to teach school, the mistress of the house at which I boarded, gave me the second volume of Mosheim's "Ecclesiastical History." It was exactly to my liking. It covered the period from Martin Luther to the end of the eighteenth century. The first volume I did not care for; because it contained the "Dark" and Middle Ages, in which there was no true Christianity! This I knew well enough. But the second volume was a treasure. I read it, and read it, over and over again. The Protestant that hugs to Mosheim will hardly discover much good in Catholicity. But at that time I knew nothing of any other Church History. For years Mosheim was to me the great and sole fountain of ecclesiastical knowledge.

How did I first learn, that any thing can be said in favor of Catholicity? I came by it in a curious way. In a village where I was teaching, the managers of the Methodist Sunday School, after holding an anniversary, sent three of their most promising scholars to Toronto, to buy books for the library. They were sent on a difficult mission: a good man might have made a mistake in his selections: they made a bad one. A few nights after the books were home, the superintendent came to me with one, and asked me whether I knew any thing about it. He said that some way it did not seem to be right. I took the book and found its title to be, "History of the Reformation," by William Cobbett! To tell the truth, I had never heard of the book before; but, concealing my ignorance of the matter as well as I could, I took it and told him that I would look through it. He appeared glad to be rid of it. That book, written by a Protestant, surprised me. It would have been more convincing to me, were its tone milder; but I saw, that the facts are honestly selected, the conclusions strictly drawn, and I carefully noted some telling quotations from Protestants, in favor of Catholicity. The book would never have made a Catholic of me, I think; but it first showed me, that Protestantism has its own black spots.

A few months later, I met a Catholic neighbor, who told me, that he had just bought Archbishop Spalding's "History of the Reformation," and that he would lend it to me. I believe that I trembled when he put it into my hands. Could I read a "Papist" book? The bare thought of doing so almost sickened me. No doubt, I should have thrown it back into his face; but I did not. I was curious to see what trash a Catholic could revel in. I read it carefully, but found nothing trashy about it. He speaks too strongly to suit a Protestant, of course; and, what is worse, he also gives quotations from Protestants, that would stagger a common Protestant. My consolation was in the hope, that, as a "Papist," he had tampered with the quotations. I would test his work. As far as I could, I did so, and found him correct in every particular. The reading of this book determined me to be a real Protestant, or, as a Protestant is often described, one who is not afraid to examine all things, to get at the truth, and who has a perfect right to judge and to decide for himself. I believed, that religion is every thing or nothing; and if every thing, too much trouble can not be taken in learning its true form.

The thought occurred to me for the first time, that my connection with Methodism was the merest accident. Had I been born a Calvinist, I should have been trained to a reverence for John of Geneva; if an Anglican, for Cranmer; if a Catholic, for Holy Church. But a dread for a moment seized me. If, what to me seemed exceedingly improbable, the Catholic Church can show a respectable record, and unfold the title deeds of her divine origin, would it be my duty to heed her? Was it my privilege to do so? Would it not be the basest ingratitude in me to turn my back on the faith of my fathers? But I saw in a moment, that, if this reproach could be cast against me, it could be cast against Luther, against Wesley himself, and against the pagan that turns to Christianity. Still, I hoped, I believed, that a careful study of these matters would confirm me in Protestantism. I had sufficient confidence in its champions to believe, that, in fair controversy, they could defend it against all Catholic assaults, and return a fire that would drive all their enemies from the field. I had nothing to fear: the cost of books was my great difficulty: the labor of the study was a pleasure.

For nearly five years, I consumed all my leisure, of which I had a great deal, in studying Church History and controversial works. Some of the principal books that I bought, I will name, not for a parade, but to show that I made a fair selection. The Protestant Church Histories were Waddington's; Smith's; Milman's "Latin Christianity," 8vols., New York, 1860; Hardwick's "Middle Ages;" Ranke's "Popes;" and (Jeremy) Collier's "Church History of England," 9vols., London, 1845: the Catholic Histories were Alzog's Ch. Hist., 3vols., Cincinnati, 1876; Butler's "Lives of the Saints;" DuPin's "History of Ecclesiastical Writers," 10vols., London, 1698; DeMontor's "Lives of the Popes;" and Gosselins' "Papal Power in the Middle Ages." To many Protestant books I added Boultbee's "Thirty-Nine Articles;" Pearson's "Creed;" and Palmer's "Church," 2vols., London, 1838. The chief Catholic books on controversy that I procured were Milner's "End;" Bossuet's "Variations;" Balmez's "Protestantism and Catholicity;" Mœhler's "Symbolism;" Fredet's "Eucharistic Mystery;" Kenrick's "Primacy;" and Wilberforce's "Church Authority."

Before I proceed to give the results of my five years' study, I will notice that I received no advice from priest or preacher. As for a priest, I had not even spoken to one. I worked alone and privately. Only he who has engaged in a labor of the kind can form the faintest idea of the hard mental strain incident to such an undertaking —the collation of authorities to prove a disputed fact; the bulk of reading necessary to dispel a hostile coloring; the close searching scrutiny to detect the lurking sophism; and above all the struggle for that commanding range of view that must be attained, to form a just and final judgment. And what is my reward? It is that I am now sure of my footing: I know for an absolute certainty that I am at last a member of the One, Holy, Catholic, and Apostolic Church.

LETTER II.

PERSECUTION.

The greatest objection against the Catholic Church, that I had always harbored, was, that she has ever been an unrelenting persecutor of all who have differed from her in faith. I had been taught to believe, that her horrid butcheries have stained with blood the pages of history; and that, had she the power to-day, she would not allow a Protestant to live. The persecution of heretics is with her a sacred work: their extermination, by brute force, is her great aim and object. This is no exaggeration: it is distinctly affirmed by many prominent Protestants. And the speakers and writers that cast against her this crowning reproach of sanguinary persecution never forget to dose their dupes with the ridiculous offset that Protestantism is essentially tolerant If I once believed such an abominable reversal of the truth, is there any excuse for me? I offer the only one I can give; it is that I was the simple dupe of those who have a bread-and-butter interest in perverting history. But how do they so completely blind people? They could do it in no way but by giving all they say a religious coloring. When one of these self-dubbed divines counterfeits the sanctity of a saint, and interlards his discourse with the pietistic phraseology of a dying mystic, he obtains the credit due to a special messenger from heaven. One of his ostentatious piety *must* speak the truth. To discredit his statements, however extravagant or vindictive they may be, would be tantamount to the rankest infidelity.

But the time came when I concluded, I would study for myself the subject of religious persecution. Perhaps, though, I took the wrong books? There may be something in this. Had I confined myself to books issued by a society whose existence depends upon the maintenance of Protestantism, or to the ponderous lucubrations of some superannuated Sunday school teacher or worn-out colporteur, I might be still one of those that "love truth for truth's sake." But, even in selecting books of history, I gave full play to my wayward nature, by taking standard, and mostly Protestant, authors. I had two questions to solve: Has the Catholic Church been the persecutor that her enemies declare her to have been? And have Protestants been the charitable, tolerant saints, that so many of their admirers so roundly assert?

When the Church first appeared in history, she appeared as a helpless sufferer. The world arrayed itself against her to destroy her. For century after century, she gave to martyrdom the ablest and the best of her children. Fathers, Saints, and Popes, submissively but triumphantly, endured the most excruciating tortures and agonizing deaths; and, instead of resisting or reviling, they prayed for the conversion of their persecutors. Exile was the mildest punishment for the defenders of the faith against Arianism; in Africa the Circumcelliones visited with death all the Catholics beyond the protection of the imperial guards; and Milman says, that even Nestorius in Constantinople "when in power, scrupled not to persecute." In short, history, when carefully examined, shows that almost the first move of those who go out of the Church, is, when they are strong enough, to wage against her actual warfare. The early heretics did so; the Manichean heretics of the Middle Ages did so; and it will be seen whether the Protestants have done so or not.

If the Church has been a persecutor, where is the first proof of it to be found? Tertullian's saying, "It does not belong to religion to force religion" (*Non est religionis cogere religionem,*) has always been the maxim of the Church. Instead of claiming the right to persecute, she expressly disclaims it. If she has persecuted, she has acted contrary to her solemn profession. Again I ask, where is the proof that she has been a persecutor? I have looked for it in vain. Milman, in his "Latin Christianity," says: "The blood of the Spanish Bishop Priscillian, the first martyr of heresy, as usual had flowed in vain. He had been put to death by the usurper Maximus, at the instigation of two other Spanish prelates, Ithacius and Valens; but to the undisguised horror of such Churchmen as Ambrose and Martin of Tours." (Vol. I. p. 276.) It can hardly be said, that the Church approved of this, unless it can be shown that all the transgressions of Catholics are countenanced by her. Whenever Catholics have persecuted, they have acted in direct contravention to the lessons of Christian forbearance and mercy, taught by the Church. If the Church has so thirsted for the blood of heretics, how did Gotteschalcus and Berengarius, both arch heretics, escape at a time when her authority in temporal matters was at its highest pitch? When her ablest enemies attempt to fix upon her the stigma of having been a ruthless persecutor, they pitch upon the Third Canon of the Fourth Lateran Council; but Collier says: "But here it must be said, that this chapter or canon is not to be found in the Mazerine copy, coeval with the council, but is transcribed from a later record." (Vol. II. p. 421.)

It will be impossible to include in a letter particular notices of the Inquisition, St. Bartholomew's day, etc., because there is considerable to be said on another side of the subject. But I have read everything within my reach that bears on them, without being able to see that the Church has been a persecutor. Catholics have persecuted, I know; but the Church, *never*. But how do Protestants appear in history? It will be useless for me to say, that they have been persecutors; nor do I need to say so. Protestants themselves shall give testimony in the case.

Gibbon, whose inveterate hostility to the Church is well known, says, in his History: "The patriot reformers were ambitious of succeeding the tyrants whom they had dethroned. They imposed with equal rigor their creeds and confessions; they asserted the right of the magistrate to punish heretics with death. The pious or personal animosity of Calvin proscribed in Servetus the guilt of his own rebellion; and the flames of Smithfield, in which he was afterwards consumed, had been kindled for the Anabaptists by the zeal of Cranmer." (Vol. v. p. 401.)

"The difference in this respect (Toleration) between the Catholics and Protestants was only in degree, and in degree there was much less difference than we are apt to believe. *Persecution is the deadly original sin of the reformed churches;* that which cools every honest man's zeal for their cause, in proportion as his reading becomes more extensive." (Hallam's Const. Hist. of Eng., Vol. i. p. 130.)

"What are the reproaches constantly applied to the Reformation by its enemies? which of its results are thrown in its face, as it were, unanswerable? The two principal reproaches are, first, the multiplicity of sects, the excessive license of thought, the destruction of all spiritual authority, and the entire dissolution of religious society: secondly, tyranny and persecution. 'You provoke licentiousness,' it has been said to the Reformers: 'you produced it; and, after having been the cause of it, you wish to restrain and repress it. And how do you repress it? By the most harsh and violent means. You take upon yourselves, too, to punish heresy, and that by virtue of an illegitimate authority.' If we take a review of all the principal charges which have been made against the Reformation, we shall find, if we set aside all questions purely doctrinal, that the above are the two fundamental reproaches to which they may be all reduced. These charges gave great embarrassment to the reform party. When they were taxed with the multiplicity of their sects, instead of advocating the freedom of religious opinion, and maintaining the right of every sect to entire toleration, they denounced sectarianism, lamented it, and endeavored to find excuses for its existence. Were they accused of persecution? They were troubled to defend themselves; they used the plea of necessity; they had, they said, the right to repress and punish error, because they were in possession of the truth. Their articles of belief, they contended, and their institutions, were the only legitimate ones; and if the Church of Rome had not the right to punish the reform party, it was because she was in the wrong and they in the right. And when the charge of persecution was applied to the ruling party in the Reformation, not by its enemies, but by its own offspring; when the sects denounced by that party said, 'We are doing just what you did; we separate ourselves from you, just as you separated yourselves from the Church of Rome,' this ruling party were still more at a loss to find an answer, and frequently the only answer they had to give was an increase of severity." (Guizot's "History of Civilization," p. 229.)

Even Mosheim says: "For every impartial and attentive observer of the rise and progress of the Reformation will ingenuously acknowledge, that wisdom and prudence did not always attend the transactions of those that were concerned in this glorious cause(!); that many things were done with violence, temerity, and precipitation; and, what is still worse, that several of the principal agents in this great revolution were actuated more by the impulse of passions, and views of interest, than by zeal for the advancement of true religion." (Vol. IV. p. 134.—Edinburgh Edition of 1819.)

"Far from evincing a tolerant spirit toward the Roman Catholics, when it was in their power, they (Lutherans) even oppressed the Calvinists: who indeed just as little deserved toeration, since they were unwilling to practice it." (Schiller's "Thirty Years' War," p. 14.)

"Kepler (d. 1631), who, while listening to the harmonies of the universe, investigated the laws of the planetary motions that he might with devout joy make known to others the miracles of divine wisdom, and would rather starve than apostatize from the Confession of Augsburg, was driven from the Lord's fold as an unsound sheep, because he would not subscribe the articles in which the Calvinists were condemned, and doubted whether the body of Christ was truly omnipresent. His mother also died in fetters under the accusation of being a witch." (Hase's Ch. Hist. p. 411.)

"We cannot but remember that libels-scarcely less scandalous than those of Herbert, mummeries scarcely less absurd than those of Clootz, and crimes scarcely less atrocious than those of Marat, disgrace the early history of Protestantism." (Macaulay's "Essays," Vol. I. p. 227.)

Speaking of the principle of persecution, held by the 'Reformers,' Palmer says: "Accordingly, they *acted* on this principle. The Lutherans rejected the Zuinglians from all communion, because they were heretical in the doctrine of the eucharist. The Calvinists in the Synod of Dort condemned and excommunicated the Arminians as heretics. The Swedish Lutherans excommunicated as heretics the Sacramentarians and the Papists. Nor was this all. They asserted the right of the civil magistrate to interfere for the suppression of heresy. This doctrine is maintained by the Helvetic, Scottish, Belgic, and Saxon Confessions; and they were so far influenced by their dread and hatred of heresy, and by the false principle of the lawfulness of inflicting capital punishment on those who were guilty of that crime, that too many instances are to be found of the execution of heretics. The cases of Servetus, Valentinus Gentilis, Campanus, Gruet, Crellius, Felix Mans, etc., are unhappily but too well known; not to speak of the imprisonment and banishment of a great number of others." ("Church," Vol. I. p. 380.) In the same volume, p. 500, he says: "In fact the writ, 'de Hæretico comburendo' was in force till the twenty-ninth year of Charles II., and not unfrequently acted upon."

Lecky in his "Rationalism in Europe," says: "Persecution among the early Protestants was a distinct and definite doctrine, digested into elaborate treatises, indissolubly connected with a large portion of the received theology, developed by the most enlightened and far-seeing theologians, and enforced against the most inoffensive as against the most formidable sects. It was the doctrine of the palmiest days of Protestantism." (Vol, II. p. 61.)

In England the Presbyterian Cartwright voiced his sentiments thus: "I deny that upon repentance there ought to follow any pardon of death.... Heretics ought to be put to death now. If this be bloody and extreme, I am content to be so counted with the Holy Ghost." (Green's "History of the English People," p. 463.)

If the Protestants had one dogma, then, common to themselves, it was, that heretics must be put to death; and it was in England particularly, that they gave practical effect to it. Protestantism had no hold upon the people of England before Elizabeth's time; a few had toyed with it as with an odd novelty, and others had used it to enrich themselves, but it is well known, that at Elizabeth's accession the nation was Catholic. She, however, had a prudential reason for not being one; and she was determined that the nation should be with her. In Burleigh and his like, she had good tools. The people were commanded to take for their belief the articles outlined by herself and her ministers. Obedience was rewarded: recusancy was not overlooked. Those that would be neither cajoled nor bribed to accept her form of faith, she subjected to a persecution that makes the most disgustingly brutal page of English history. Hallam shall tell what she did: " But they (Eliz. and her ministers) established a persecution which fell not at all short in principle of that for which the inquisition had become so odious." (Const. Hist. of Eng. Vol. I. p. 196.) Priests were her choice game: all that fell into her hands she brutally murdered. But how ? The form of their deaths can be surmised from the following: " Lord Bacon in his observations on a libel written against Lord Burleigh in 1592, does not deny the 'bowellings' of catholics; but makes a sort of apology for it, as 'less cruel than the wheel or forcipation, or even simple burning.' " (Id. p. 223.) In England Catholicity was trampled out in blood ; and Protestantism established by the power of a court famous for falsity, intrigue, and cruelty.

Concerning Ireland Hase says : " Whatever was done by the kings of England against the papacy and in behalf of the Reformation, was enforced also as the law for Ireland. But the Irish obstinately resisted every effort of their tyrannical oppressors to compel them to embrace the new faith. The English, however, proved from the Old Testament that as a conquered territory Ireland belonged to them as Canaan once belonged to the Israelites. The free and common territory of the confederated and kindred tribes was converted into royal fiefs, and when the principal chiefs were goaded on by continual oppressions to rise in rebellion, their lands were given to Englishmen, until the native inhabitants were almost completely destitute of property. The entire revenues and property of the Church were gradually taken possession of by a foreign Protestant hierarchy, by the side of which the Irish were obliged to sustain their own bishops and pastors from their own scanty resources." (C. H. p. 422.) And, because the Irish have steadily refused to fall away from the faith of their fathers, at the imperious dictation of their oppressors, they have, from the time of Henry VIII., labored under the hardest restraints, and have endured the direst persecutions. Read the penal laws : they are given by the Protestant Walpole, in his " History of Ireland," Bk. v. Ch. vi. " Every Catholic priest found in Ireland," says Sydney Smith, " was hanged, and five pounds paid to the informer. . . . By the Articles of Limerick, the Irish were promised the free exercise of their religion ; but from that period to the year 1788, every year produced some fresh penalty against that religion, some liberty was abridged, some right impaired, or some suffering increased. By acts in King William's reign, they were prevented from being solicitors. No Catholic was allowed to marry a Protestant ; and any Catholic who sent a son to Catholic countries for education was to forfeit all his lands. In the reign of Queen Anne, any son of a Catholic who chose to turn Protestant got possession of the father's estate. . . . Every Papist teaching schools to be presented as a regular Popish convict. Prices of catching Catholic priests, from 50s. to £10, according to rank." From the " History of Ireland," by the Protestant Leland, he extracted this : " The favorite object of the Irish Government and the English Parliament was the utter extermination of all the Catholic inhabitants of Ireland." Macaulay, in his speech on the " State of Ireland," after saying that the policy of Cromwell was " extirpation " and the policy of William III. " perhaps not more humane in reality," proceeds thus : " The Irish Roman Catholics were permitted to live, to be fruitful, to replenish the earth : but they were doomed to be what the Helots were in Sparta, what the Greeks were under the Ottoman, what the blacks now are at New York. Every man of the subject caste was strictly excluded from public trust. Take what path he might in life, he was crossed at every step by some vexatious restriction. It was only by being obscure and inactive that he could, on his native soil, be safe. If he aspired to be powerful and honored, he must begin by being an exile. If he pined for military glory, he might gain a cross or perhaps a Marshal's staff in the armies of France or Austria. If his vocation was to politics, he might distinguish himself in the diplomacy of Italy or Spain. But at home he was a mere Gibeonite, a hewer of wood and a drawer of water." In this country, though, we often hear a different version of the matter. The champions of "civil and religious liberty, etc., etc.," at their annual gatherings, describe, in the basest and profanest rhetoric, the struggles and the sufferings of their fathers in Ireland. And, if the general notion of Irish affairs be different from written history, there may be some reason for it. The majority of people have little opportunity, and perhaps less inclination, to read the history of Ireland. They gradually adopt, then, without investigation, the rank statements of some men who call themselves Irishmen. Nor can they be heavily censured for doing so; for what could more quickly win a man to the cause of justice and truth, than the regulation speech of a well-charged Orangeman, when he tussles with *facts* on the "glorious twelfth?" But true history upsets all he says, and exposes the innocence of those whom he glorifies. "The object of the Protestant faction (Peep-o'-day Boys)," says Walpole, "was to expel from the country those Roman Catholics who were scattered about among the Protestants of the north, and to occupy their holdings." He cites Lord Gosford, the governor of Armagh, for this: "Neither age nor sex, nor even acknowledged innocence as to any guilt in the late disturbances, is sufficient to excite mercy, much less to afford protection. The only crime which the objects of this ruthless persecution are charged with is simply a profession of the Roman Catholic religion. A lawless banditti (Orangemen) have constituted themselves judges of this new species of delinquency, and the sentence they have pronounced is nothing less than a confiscation of all property, and an immediate banishment." Greene, in his Hist., p. 775, says: "For a while, however, the Protestant landowners, banded together in 'Orange Societies,' held the country down by sheer terror and bloodshed. . . Ireland was in fact driven into rebellion by the lawless cruelty of the Orange yeomanry and the English troops. In 1796 and 1797 soldiers and yeomanry marched over the country torturing and scourging the 'croppies,' as the Irish insurgents were called in derision from their shortcut hair, robbing, ravishing, and murdering." Knight, (Hist. of Eng., Ch. CXCVII.), says: "The administrators of martial law were undisciplined troops of *yeomanry*, headed by ignorant and reckless officers. They made the government odious by their cruel oppressions." Sydney Smith, in Letter VII. of "Letters to Peter Plymley," rallies the Irish peasant who "allows the Orange bloodhound to ransack his cottage at pleasure." And, in Letter VIII., he concludes a paragraph with these two sentences: "To a short period of disaffection among the Orangemen I confess I should not much object: my love of poetical justice does carry me as far as that; one summer's whipping, only one: the thumb-screw for a short season; a little light easy torturing between Lady-day and Michaelmas; a short specimen of Mr. Perceval's rigor. I have malice enough to ask this slight atonement for the groans and shrieks of the poor Catholics, unheard by any human tribunal, but registered by the Angel of God against their Protestant and enlightened oppressors."

How could I read all these statements, and many others fully as strong, made by Protestants of acknowledged ability and learning, and made often with every appearance of regret and shame, without coming to the conclusion, that, whatever Catholics may have been as persecutors, the Protestants have in principle and action surpassed them. I saw that the common Protestant cry, that persecution is the singular disgrace of the Catholic Church, is a matchless instance of cool, brazen-cheeked impudence. I also saw, that, if I were to object to Catholicity for my old reason, I should have to decline Protestantism on the same account. But I might have been told, perhaps, that Protestantism has been thoroughly purified from every trace of bigotry, while the Catholics are as they have always been. This way of putting it might have checked me to a reconsideration some time ago, but now I know better; and, if any Protestant would like to test this little fancy, let him show in his religious movements any thing like absolute independence. Proofs of some kind will soon reach him.

LETTER III.

THE CHURCH AND LEARNING.

While investigating sections of history, for the purpose of learning something about persecution, I came across several scraps that have a bearing on another charge often made against the Church; namely, that it has always been her steady care and sensible interest to check every aspiration of her people towards intellectual culture. The mildest form of the statement generally made, is, that, if she has not actually exerted her authority to keep Christendom comfortably ignorant, she has studiously refrained from encouraging any effort put forth for the diffusion of knowledge. This opinion, it is safe to say, is firmly rooted in the Protestant mind. What ordinary Protestant is not certain of it? But how extraordinary it is that people passably intelligent can entertain such a contradiction of all respectable history. Of course, I was once full of it; but, after a moderate course of reading, I was forced to dissent from the popular view of the matter. And Protestants themselves turned me around.

It is conceded on all sides, that there was in Europe a decline of letters, from the time of Charlemagne to about the 10th century, though its causes had no connection whatever with the Church; but, from that time to the time of Luther, there was a steady advance made in literature and science. And it was increasingly made, too, under the protecting shadow of the Church, as her temporal influence and power became more extensive and generally acknowledged. This I gathered from such carefully weighed statements as the following, taken from Protestant writers:—

Speaking of the Eleventh and Twelfth Centuries, Hase says: "No sooner was there sufficient order secured in the state and in the Church to afford opportunity for a tranquil elevation and communion of spirit among men, than the exuberance of life which had long been concealed broke forth in the cultivation of science." (C. H. p. 236.)

"The amount of education (11th century) must have differed with the circumstances of the country, diocese, or parish: still we are assured that efforts were continually made to organize both town and village schools. The richest institutions of this class were the conventual seminaries of the French and German Benedictines; and although they often shared in the deterioration of the order (certainly), and were broken up by the invasions of the Magyars and Northmen, we must view them as the greatest boon to all succeeding ages; since in them especially the copies of the Sacred Volume, of the Fathers, and of other books were hoarded and transcribed." (Hardwick's "Middle Ages," p. 193.)

"The example of Sylvester II. (Pope 999—1003) might

be sufficient to rouse the jealous emulation of Italy; and Sylvester left to that country not his example only, but the fruits of his active zeal in encouraging the learned of his own time, and in establishing schools and collecting libraries for the use of other generations. Some of the Popes, his successors, followed his traces with more or less earnestness; and among the rest, Gregory VII. added to his extraordinary qualities the undisputed merit of promoting the progress of education." (Waddington's Ch. Hist. p. 267.)

Speaking of southern Italy, Milman, in his L. C., Vol. v. p. 392, says: "Greek was the spoken language of the people in many parts of the kingdom; the laws of Frederic were translated into Greek for popular use; the epitaph of the Archbishop of Messina in the year 1175 was Greek. There were Greek priests and Greek congregations in many parts of Apulia and Sicily; the privileges conferred by the Emperor Henry VI. on Messina had enacted that one of the three magistrates should be a Greek. Hebrew, and still more Arabic, were well known, not merely by Jews and Arabians but by learned scholars. Frederic himself spoke German, Italian, Latin, Greek, Arabic, and Hebrew." In Vol. VII., p. 355, he writes: "His (Wycliffe's) destination, either from his own choice or the wise providence of his parents, was that of a scholar, to which the humblest could in those days aspire. *England was almost a land of schools;* every Cathedral, almost every Monastery, had its own; but youths of more ambition, self-confidence, supposed capacity, and of better opportunities, thronged to Oxford and Cambridge, now in their highest repute. In England, as throughout Christendom, that wonderful rush, as it were, of a vast part of the population towards knowledge, thronged the Universities with thousands of students, instead of the few hundreds who have now the privilege of entering those seats of instruction." In Vol. VIII. p. 250, he says, "The cultivation of the Greek had never entirely ceased in the West." On the next page there is: "Towards the end of the thirteenth century the philosophers of Greece and Rome were as well known, as in our own days; the schools rung with their names, with the explanation of their writings." And, in the same volume, p. 265, he says of Albert of Cologne: "His title to fame is not that he introduced and interpreted the Metaphysics and Physics of Aristotle, and the works of the Arabian philosophers on these abstruse subjects to the world, but because he opened the field of true philosophic observation to mankind. In natural history he unfolded the more precious treasures of the Aristotelian philosophy, he revealed all the secrets of ancient science, and added large contributions of his own on every branch of it; in mathematics he commented on and explained Euclid; in chemistry, he was a subtle investigator; in astronomy, a bold speculator."

"There is a wide-spread notion that the Middle Ages were also 'Dark Ages,' full of ignorance and superstition, with hardly a ray of knowledge or true religion to enlighten the gloom, and also that the Church was the great encourager of this state of things; indeed, that it was mainly due to the influence of the monks and of the Clergy generally. This belief is however quite unhistorical. . . Thus not only theology, but secular knowlege besides, found a home in the Church, which was at once the guardian and the channel of literature. . . The Mediæval Church was, in reality, a great supporter of learning." ("Key to Church History," by John H. Blunt, M. A., pp. 115—117.)

Of the eleventh century, Mosheim says: "This vehement desire of knowledge, that increased from day to day, and became, at length, the predominant passion of the politest European nations, produced many happy effects. To it, more particularly, we must attribute the considerable number of public schools that were opened in various places, and the choice of more able and eminent masters, than those who had formerly presided in the seminaries of learning. Towards the conclusion of the preceding age, there were no schools in Europe but those which belonged to monasteries, or episcopal residences, nor were there any other masters, except the Benedictine monks, to instruct the youth in the principles of sacred and profane erudition. But, not long after the commencement of this century, the face of things was totally changed, and that in a manner the most advantageous to the cause of letters." (Vol. II. p. 461.) Of the twelfth century, he says: "In the western world the pursuit of knowledge was now carried on with incredible emulation and ardour, and all the various branches of science were studied with the greatest application and industry. This literary enthusiasm was encouraged and supported by the influence and liberality of certain of the European monarchs, and Roman pontiffs, who perceived the happy tendency of the sciences to soften the savage manners of uncivilized nations, and thereby to administer an additional support to civil government, as well as an ornament to human society. Hence learned societies were formed, and colleges established in several places, in which the liberal arts and sciences were publicly taught." (Vol. III. p. 28.) In the thirteenth century, he says: "The sciences carried a fairer aspect in the western world, where every branch of erudition was cultivated with assiduity and zeal, and, of consequence, flourished, with increasing vigour, from day to day. . . The industrious youth either applied themselves entirely to the study of the civil and canon laws, which was a sure path to preferment, or employed their labours in philosophical researches, in order to the attainment of a shining reputation, and of the applause that was lavished upon such as were endowed with a subtile and metaphysical genius.

Hence the bitter complaints that were made by the pontiffs and other bishops, of the neglect and decline of the liberal arts and sciences; and hence also the zealous, but unsuccessful efforts they used to turn the youth from jurisprudence and philosophy, to the study of humanity and philology." (Vol. III. pp. 150—154.) And, of the fourteenth century, he says: "In all the Latin provinces, schemes were laid and carried into execution with considerable success, for promoting the study of letters, improving taste, and dispelling the pedantic spirit of the times. This laudable disposition gave rise to the election of many schools and academies, at *Cologn*, *Orleans*, *Cahors*, *Perusia*, *Florence*, and *Pisa*, in which all the liberal arts and sciences, distributed into the same classes that still subsist in those places, were taught with assiduity and zeal. Opulent persons founded and amply endowed particular colleges, in the public universities, in which, besides the monks, young men of narrow circumstances were educated in all the branches of literature. Libraries were also collected, and men of learning animated to aspire to fame and glory, by the prospect of honourable rewards... Clement V. who was now raised to the pontificate, ordered the Hebrew, and other Oriental languages, to be taught in the public schools, that the Church might never want a sufficient number of missionaries properly qualified to dispute with the Jews and Mahometans, and to diffuse the divine light of the gospel throughout the east: in consequence of which appointment, some eminent proficients in these tongues, and especially in the Hebrew, flourished during this age." (Vol. III. pp. 305—306.)

"It might, I think, be shewn that there were a good many persons in those ages not so destitute of all that is now called learning as some have asserted; and many without inquiry believe. I might ask, how does it happen that the classics, and the older works on art or science, have been preserved in existence? and I might with still greater force (but obviously with intolerable prolixity), appeal to the works of writers of those ages to show that they knew the meaning of that which, no one can deny, they preserved and multiplied." ("Dark Ages," by Rev. S. R. Maitland, F.R.S. & F.S.A., p. 173—Ed. of 1844.)

Commenting on the period subsequent to Gregory VII., the Catholic historian Alzog says: "In the cloister-schools and cathedral-schools, excellent masters were provided to impart gratuitous education to all comers, and forbidden to receive any compensation for their labor. So rapid was the advance of the intellect, and so great the demand for mental training, that schools of inferior note were soon transformed into *universities*, without, however, at once embracing in their scope the full curriculum of scientific studies. Some taught more, some fewer branches, and each had its speciality. At *Salerno*, it was medicine; at *Bologna* (1200), jurisprudence, and at *Paris* (1206), canon law, dialectics, and theology. *The mutual interdependence of the four leading branches of science was recognized and appreciated.*" (Ch. Hist., Vol. II. p. 729.) In a foot-note on the same page, he adds: "In addition to these three universities, we have to count the following, which sprang up, one after another: 1. In *Italy*—Vicenza, 1204; Padua, 1222; Naples, 1224; Vercelli, 1228; Piacenza, 1246; Treviso, 1260; Ferrara (1264), 139N; Perugia, 1276; Rome, 1303; Pisa, 1343, and reestablished in 1472; Pavia, 1361; Palermo, 1394; Turin, 1405; Cremona, 1413; Florence, 1438; Catanea, 1445. 2. In *France*—Montpellier (1180), 1289; Toulouse, 1228; Lyons, 1300; Cahors, 1332; Avignon, 1340; Angers, 1364; Aix, 1409; Caen, 1430 (1450); Bordeaux, 1441; Valence, 1452; Nantes, 1463; Bourges, 1465. 3. In *Portugal* and *Spain*—Salamanca, 1240; Lisbon (translated to Coimbra), 1290; Valladolid, 1346; Huesca, 1354; Valencia, 1410; Siguenza, 1471; Saragossa, 1474; Avila, 1482; Alcala, 1499 (1508); Seville, 1504. 4. In

England—Oxford, 1249; Cambridge, 1257. 5. In *Scotland*—St. Andrews, 1412; Glasgow, 1454; Aberdeen, 1477. 6. In *Burgundy*—Dole, 1426. 7. In *Brabant*—Louvain,———. 8. In *Germany*—Vienna, 1365; Heidelberg, 1386; Cologne, 1388; Erfurt, 1392; Ingolstadt, 1401; Wurzburg, 1403; Leipsig, 1409; Rostock, 1419; Greifswalde, 1456; Freiburg, 1457 (opened April 26, 1460); Basle, 1460; Treves, 1472; Tubingen, 1456; Mentz, 1477; Wittenberg, 1502; Frankfort on the Oder, 1506. 9. In *Bohemia*—Prague, 1347. 10. In *Poland*—Cracow (1347), 1400. 11. In *Denmark*—Copenhagen. 12. In *Sweden*—Upsala, 1477. 13. In *Hungary*—Funfkirchen, 1367; Ofen (Buda), 1465; Presburg, 1467. 14. In *Ireland*—Dublin, 1320 (1591, 1592)."

All these express testimonies to the prevalence of education in the Middle Ages, and many others that I could transcribe, if space permitted, convinced me, that during Catholic times there were schools and teachers in abundance; and besides that the best education of the time, and no age can give a better, was the boon of every poor lad that had the spirit to work for it. In those times there were free schools for all. Free schools in the Middle Ages! Protestants that have investigated the matter frankly admit it. And that every young man, during Catholic times, could get a good education can be readily inferred from the common accounts given of the foremost men, about the time of Luther. Who was Bucer?—the son of a very poor Jew. Who was Chemnitz?—the son of a wool-comber. Who was Osiander?—the son of a blacksmith. Who was Reuchlin, the famous Hebrew scholar?—the son of very poor parents. Who was Erasmus?—a waif educated by a monastic order. Who was Melancthon?—the son of an armorer. Who was Luther himself?—the son of a common miner. We are told, that Luther, who received a Catholic education, was a prime Latinist and a fair Grecian, when only twelve years old.

Compare this with the vulgar report, that the great aim of the Catholics has been to keep poor people in ignorance. One thing I know well, that, if Luther had been a Cornish miner's son, in the beginning of the 19th century, instead of a German miner's son, at the beginning of the 16th century, his name would never be seen in history. Since the "glorious Reformation," few miners' sons, in Cornwall, have seen much of the schoolmaster's face; they have learned more about washing tin than construing Latin. True enough, a few favored ones have sometimes managed to pick up, in sundry ways and divers forms, a little reading, some writing, and less arithmetic; but the majority have had to be contented with much less. It was lucky for Luther that he was not born in a Protestant country.

These facts and considerations satisfied me, that railing at Catholics for checking mental progress, and at the same time applauding Protestants for giving a knowledge of letters to the world, is a matchless instance of contemptible ignorance. But it is still insisted upon by certain classes of professional men. One of them is the hungry orator that hovers around socials and picnics, in quest of free meals. The "Dark Ages" is often his favorite theme. To him it is an indefinite period and a profoundly dark one; but, if he knows nothing about the subject, he knows his audience. One of his expressions is "the intellectual stupor of the Dark Ages;" he calls "the education of the masses" the product and patronised adjunct of Protestantism. His discourse is a medley of historical errors, stale yarns, and expressions of contempt for the ignorant old people that used to live upon the earth. His audience, those who boast of freedom of enquiry, suck in the whole mess, and never trouble themselves with once looking into the matter, to try his statements. So error is propagated and preserved.

LETTER IV.

MONASTICISM.

Few institutions connected with the Church have been more falsely described or foully defamed than the monastic orders. Since the time of Henry VIII., when, for the sake of pure and wholesale plunder, the vilest accusations that the most sordid natures could conceive were trumped up against them, few historians have dared open their case to the world, or speak a word in their behalf. Those that shared in plundering them, and were thereby raised from cringing indigence to fat landlordism, have never ceased in villifying the monks, and holding them up to derision and contempt. They were lazy, besotted beings, cumberers of the ground, having their bellies always full and their bodies always filthy. On the stage, in novels, in graver books called history, in every picture into which he could be dragged, the monk has been caricatured. But, if the monks were so contemptible, have not unnecessary pains been taken in dishonoring them? After being robbed of their property and thrown upon the charity of a world whose passions had been inflamed against them, would it not have been simply decent to let the poor monks die in peace? But too much calumny made men suspicious. Honester men arose, who carefully and temperately looked into the history of monasticism, and then some justice was done to the monks.

Hence, for a long time it has been considered a sign of enlightenment, to affect a contempt for everything relating to monasticism; but I am proud to say, that, although I had no specific reason for it, I always had a lurking reverence for a monk. A Catholic no doubt he was, and a good one; but for all that there was an indefinable something in him that I secretly admired: and I have often wondered how it was, that I, who had been trained to the deepest hatred of Catholicity, could yet hold something akin to affection for the most active members of its militia. Often I took fancy flights into the times when they were in their might and splendor, and conjured up pretty pictures of their grand old buildings and their surroundings. But nothing could be more imaginary; for I knew nothing, or next to nothing, about them. As long ago as I can remember, I had a burning wish to know the history of the Benedictines and their off-shoots; but, for years and years, I could not discover where a book on the subject could be found, or whether there was a work of the kind in existence or not. I remember asking a very intelligent clergyman, whether he knew of such a book, but he could give me no satisfactory answer: and it was only when I came across a catalogue of Catholic books, that I found out that the work I had longed for is Montalembert's "Monks of the West." I got it at once, and gave it a thorough study. This is the indispensable work, in English, for a full and correct knowledge of monasticism. It is a noble work—an ornament to any library. It describes the origin of monasticism, traces its history until it became a settled system, fully analyzes its aims, and estimates its capabilities for mission work; it shows how the free-holdings of waste or wild lands, given to a single monk or to a small body of monks, were settled on, cleared up, and thoroughly cultivated and embellished with those imposing edifices whose present ruins are a tantalizing defiance to the architectural skill of the monks' modern traducers; it demonstrates, with a fullness of proof, that the indefeasible title of the monks to those possessions rested on the double ground of the original grant and the labors of the pioneer; it notices besides, that, although monasticism was never designed for creating scientists and literati, yet the pursuit of the studies that make such men has engaged the attention of many clever, hooded brothers, and that, through their unwearied diligence and happy methods of generalization, the sciences were materially advanced, and letters not only cultivated and taught in thousands of schools, but collected and preserved, to be handed on for, too often, ungrateful generations of the future; but more especially it points out, that it is to the undying honor of the monks, that, during the turbulent periods of the Middle Ages, they always gave an asylum to the helpless and destitute, succored the needy, relieved the poor, gave the warmest hospitality to the stranger, nourished the sick, braved every form of infection and plague to soothe the pillow of the dying, and, by their earnest, gentle demeanor and sympathizing conduct, communicated to the oppressed and wronged that sustaining hope of future happiness that turns the trials of this world into disciplinary blessings. And all this can be gathered from the following Protestant admissions:

"It is quite impossible to touch the subject of MONASTICISM without rubbing off some of the dirt which has been heaped upon it. It is impossible to get even a superficial knowledge of the mediæval history of Europe, without seeing how greatly the world of that period was indebted to the Monastic Orders; and feeling that, whether they were good or bad in other matters, monasteries were beyond all price in those days of misrule and turbulence, as places where (it may be imperfectly, yet better than elsewhere) God was worshipped—as a quiet and religious refuge for helpless infancy and old age, a shelter of respectful sympathy for the orphan maiden and the desolate widow— as central points whence agriculture was to spread over bleak hills, and barren downs, and marshy plains, and deal its bread to millions perishing with hunger and its pestilential train—as repositories of the learning which then was, and well-springs for the learning which was to be—as nurseries of art and science, giving the stimulus, the means, and the reward to invention, and aggregating around them every head that could devise, and every hand that could execute—as the nucleus of the city which in after-days of pride should crown its palaces and bulwarks with the towering cross of its cathedral.

"This I think no man can deny. I believe it is true, and I love to think of it. I hope that I see the good hand of God in it, and the visible trace of his mercy that is over all his works. But if it is only a dream, however grateful, I shall be glad to be awakened from it; not indeed by the yelling of illiterate agitators, but by a quiet and sober proof that I have misunderstood the matter. In the mean time, let me thankfully believe that thousands of the persons at whom Robertson, and Jortin, and other such very miserable second-hand writers, have sneered at, were men of enlarged minds, purified affections, and holy lives—that they were justly reverenced by men—and, above all, favourably accepted by God, and distinguished by the highest honour which He vouchsafes to those whom He has called into existence, that of being the channels of his love and mercy to their fellow-creatures." (Maitland's D. A., p. iv.)

"It is not easy to estimate the vast amount of good which the labours of the Benedictine monks conferred on the Church of the Middle Ages, good which has left many traces to the present day. Not only did they provide in a vast number of instances for the spiritual wants of the parishes in and near which they lived, as well as for the education of the young, *both rich and poor*, but they were also the philosophers, the authors, the artists, and the physicians, nay, even the farmers and the mechanics of Mediaeval times. They built cathedrals and churches, made roads and bridges, copied books when writing stood in the place of printing, and were in general the props and pioneers of civilization." (Blunt's Key to C. H. p. 112.)

"The Benedictines preserved the monuments of antiquity for a more cultivated age, made the deserts fertile, and became the instructors of the people." (Hase's C. H., p. 151.)

Hardwick can hardly forgive the monks for their loyalty to the Papacy; but stubborn facts elicited from him the acknowledgment, that the order of St. Benedict "must notwithstanding be regarded as a patron of the arts, and as contributing to fan the embers of religion." (M. A., p, 44.)

"Yet the curiosity or zeal of some learned solitaries has cultivated the ecclesiastical, and even the profane, sciences; and posterity must gratefully acknowledge, that the monuments of Greek and Roman literature have been preserved and multiplied by their indefatigable pens." (Gibbon's Hist., Vol. III. p. 533.) And, in Vol. VI. p. 13, he says: "A philosophic age has abolished, with too liberal and indiscriminate disdain, the honors of these spiritual heroes."

"And we say, properly enough, that the men of the Middle Ages, for example, speak to us by the great architectural works which they have left behind them, and which tell us very plainly of their genius, their piety, and their valor." (Whitney's " Life and Growth of Language," p. 1.)

The following is taken from Montalembert's "Monks of the West:" "They (monks) were permanent mediators between the rich and poor, between the strong and the weak; and it must be said to their eternal honor that they understood and fulfilled, in a marvelous way, the duties of this noble mission. They alone had the right and the means of arresting the rough hand of power, of mitigating the just severity of the law, of showing a gleam of hope to the eye of the slave, and of finding, even in this world, a place and means of existence for all those forsaken ones whose existence was ignored by the state." (Kemble's "Saxons in England," Vol. II. p. 375.)

"But it would equally be unjust to assert, that establishments of pious men, associated for religious purposes, were without their use in exciting respect in the enemy (pagans), and confidence in the Christian. Still less can we hesitate to believe, that they were the means of relieving much individual misery; that during the overthrow of justice and humanity, they derived power, as well as protection, from the name of God, and from the trust which they reposed in Him; that their power was generally exerted for good purposes; and that their gates were thrown open to multitudes, who, in those days of universal desolation, could hope for no other refuge." (Waddington's Ch. Hist. p. 305.)

"The Christianity of the Anglo-Saxon kingdoms, whether from Rome or Iona, was alike monastic. That form of the religion already prevailed in Britain, when invaded by the Saxons, with them retreated into Wales, or found refuge in Ireland. It landed with Augustine on the shores of Kent; and came back again, on the invitation of the Northumbrian king, from the Scottish isles. And no form of Christianity could be so well suited for its high purposes at that time, or tend so powerfully to promote civilization as well as religion.

"The calm example of the domestic virtues in a more polished, but often, as regards sexual intercourse more corrupt state of morals, is of inestimable value, as spreading around the parsonage an atmosphere of peace and happiness (albeit in the shade of a parasol), and offering a living lesson on the blessings of conjugal fidelity. But such Christianity would have made no impression, even if it could have existed, on a people who still retained something of their Teutonic severity of manners, and required therefore something more imposing—a sterner and more manifest self-denial—to keep up their religious veneration. The detachment of the clergy from all earthly ties left them at once more unremittingly devoted to their unsettled life as missionaries, more ready to encounter the perils of this wild age; while (at the same time) the rude minds of the people were more struck by their unusual habits, by the strength of character shown in their labors, their mortifications, their fastings, and perpetual religious services." (Milman's L. C., Vol. II. p. 205.) If an anti-celibate should happen to read this, let him give it a second perusal and then digest it at his leisure.

"The advantages accruing to the public from these religious houses were considerable, upon several accounts. To mention some of them: the temporal nobility and gentry had a creditable way of providing for their younger children. Those who were disposed to withdraw from the world, or not likely to make their fortunes in it, had a handsome retreat to the cloister. Here they were furnished with conveniences for life and study, with opportunities for thought and recollection, and over and above passed their time in a condition not unbecoming their quality. The charge of the family being thus lessened, there was no temptation for racking of tenants; no occasion for breaking the bulk of the estate to provide for the younger children. Thus figure and good housekeeping were maintained with greater ease, the entireness of the estate, and by consequence the lasting of the family better secured. It is true, there were sometimes small sums given to the monasteries for admitting persons to be professed; but, generally speaking, they received them gratis. This they thought most advisable, to cultivate an interest with persons of condition. By this means, they engaged great families to appear for them, upon occasion, both at court and in parliament.

"The abbeys were very serviceable places for the education of young people: every convent had one person or more assigned for this business. Thus the children of the neighborhood were taught grammar and music without any charge to their parents: and in the nunneries those of the other sex learned to work, and read English, with some advances into Latin; and particularly the nunnery at Godstow, in Oxfordshire, was famous upon this account, and for breeding young gentlewomen and others to improvements proper to their condition.

"Further, it is to the abbeys we are obliged for most of our historians, both of Church and State: these places of retirement had both most learning and leisure for such undertakings: neither did they want information for such employment: for not to mention several episcopal sees were founded for the cloister, the mitred abbots, as we have seen, sat in parliament, and not a few of the religious had a share in the convocation. It is not denied but that they were some of the best landlords. Their reserved rents were low, and their fines easy: and sometimes the product of the farms, without paying money, discharged the tenants in a great measure. They were particularly remarkable for their hospitality. The monasteries were, as it were, houses of public entertainment for the gentry that travelled: and as for their distributions of charity, it may be guessed from one instance. While the religious houses were standing, there were no provisions of parliament to relieve the poor: no assessment upon the parish for that purpose. But now this charge upon the kingdom amounts at a moderate computation, to 800,000*l.* per annum." (Collier's Hist., Vol. v. p. 28.) On page 30, of the same volume, he says: "The founders had the benefit of corrodies: that is, they had the privilege of quartering a certain number of poor servants upon the abbeys. Thus people that were worn out with age and labour, and in no condition to support themselves, were not left to starving or parish collections, but had a comfortable retreat to the abbeys, where they were maintained without hardship or marks of indigence during life. . . .

"Another misfortune consequent upon the suppression of the abbeys, was an ignorant destruction of a great many valuable books: most of the learned records of that age were lodged in the monasteries. Printing was then but a late invention, and had secured but a few books in comparison of the rest. The main of learning lay in manuscripts, and the most considerable of these both for number and quality, were in the monks' possession. But the abbeys, at their dissolution falling oftentimes into hands who understood no further than the estates, the libraries were miserably disposed of. The books, instead of being removed to royal libraries, to those of cathedrals, or the universities, were frequently thrown in to the guarantees, as things of slender consideration. Now these men oftentimes proved a very ill protection for learning and antiquity. Their avarice was sometimes so mean, and their ignorance so undistinguishing, that when the covers were somewhat rich, and would yield a little, they pulled them off, threw away the books, or turned them to waste paper. Thus many noble manuscripts were destroyed, to a public scandal, and an irreparable loss of learning."

"English architecture may be said to owe its origin to ecclesiastical bodies, not only because they required extensive places of worship for their use, and were possessed of wealth adequate to their construction, but the designs and execution of the work itself were frequently furnished by the members of monastic fraternities. The whole of the book learning of the country was in their hands; and to this they added those arts which are connected with ornamenting MSS., artificial penmanship, and minute painting and gilding for illuminations. Their talents were also often directed to objects of more obvious and immediate use; for they frequently superintended certain species of manufactures within their walls, and converted the raw material with which their lands furnished them into articles ready for the market. In all this, the sanctity which was attached to the religious body answered the great end of all political institutions, the security of property; and at a period when every other tenure was uncertain, religion .... provided a safeguard against violence, which enabled the monastic orders to cultivate the substantial good of the country." ("History of the Church of England," by Thos. V. Short, D.D.,—p. 136.)

But on the supposition, nothing more mind, that the monasteries had become lax in discipline, or their inmates addicted to occasional immoralities, were these justifiable reasons for their plunder? Let Collier answer: "If degeneracy and misbehaviour were the grand motive for dissolution, why were they not put under a better management? Why had they not some trial for reformation? If unnecessary expense, and omission of kindness to the poor, if luxury and license are good reasons to change the owner, and determine the estate,—if this will hold, we should have strange transferring of titles. At this rate, it is to be feared, some people would have a very slender claim to their abbey-lands." (Vol. v. p. 19.) He probably had in his mind the spoliation of the monasteries, when he wrote: "Had the English laity not enriched themselves with the spoils of the Church, the Reformation would have had a clearer complexion, and been better understood by the rest of Christendom; but when Protestancy had such a face of interest,—when men got manors and townships by renouncing the pope,—when people of slender pretensions made estates out of their orthodoxy, and shot up into title and figure, when the Church was stripped of her revenues, and maimed in her jurisdiction, —when changes in religion were carried on by revolt and civil commotion, as it happened in France, Scotland, and the Low Countries,—when they saw discipline laid asleep, learning decay, and liberty (license) increase, these were discouraging circumstances." (Vol. v. p. 21.) On page

25, of the same volume, he says, "The suppression of abbeys was generally disliked." And Short, on the 224th page of his Hist., scruples not to say, that "the general plan of the Reformation was of making a gain of godliness."

A good many Protestants, though, who make admissions to the general worth of monasticism, seem to be afflicted with the dread, that in some mysterious way they have committed themselves to something which, unless smirched somehow, will scarcely be acceptable to a fastidious public. Unqualified praise of "monkery" would never do. Besides, it was too closely allied to the Church to be exactly right. Now, what is the great and final condemnation of monasticism? *Risum teneatis, amici!* It was good only for the times during which it flourished! But these men never point to the agencies that have been instituted, since its suppression, for doing the work which all allow the monks did so well. What provision have the great economists made for giving relief to the poor and the helpless? Here and there, throughout England, they have established poor-houses, in some places called "Unions,"—miserable dens, where the inmates are half starved, upbraided for their misfortunes, and made the sport of their brutal keepers.

For nearly three hundred years, did Protestant England do any thing towards the education of the common people? Do not forget it, now; when the English were Catholics, the poorest in the land could get the same monastic education as the richest. Since the suppression of the monasteries, what institutions have there been for educating the poor? None at all. So far as getting an education goes, a poor boy might about as well have been in the heart of Africa as in Protestant England. When the monastic lands and chantry lands were under Catholic management, any man could get a lease under easy conditions, and maintain himself and his family respectably.

Since these domains have been in the hand of the despoilers, the bulk of the people have lived as serfs, while the favored few that have been renters have hardly been able, by practising every species of niggardliness, to scrape enough together to satisfy the inexorable landlord. In what way, now, has the worldly condition of the people been improved? "Yes, yes," says the zealous Protestant, "the worldly condition is what most concerns you; religion is the great consideration with me." And very often, in a moment of forgetfulness or through ignorance, he refers you to the grand old churches and cathedrals, that are the ornament and pride of England, as monuments to the honor and glory of his religion! In one of these glorious edifices, that has been internally vandalized, he can sit and worship, and join in the chorus of invective, launched against the memory of the very men that put over him the covering from the weather—the monks.

When I think of the monasteries and the monks, I think of England, and of the time when, as Milman says, "England was almost a land of schools," and when, as Collier says, "the children of the neighborhood were taught grammar and music without any charge to their parents," and I frankly confess, that, when the subject comes into my mind, I am troubled with vexatious reflections. I entertain the peculiar crotchet, that, had the early "reformers" been more taken up with "the gospel" and kept a little more in abeyance their craving for plunder, in one at least of the old monasteries that used to be in Cornwall, I might have been well drilled, when a boy, in the elements of a good education. In the matter of an education, how has the "Reformation" benefited me? I ask my relations. How have the common people of England been so greatly benefited? I ask everybody. And when I see an old-country man whose whole school course was worked out, in three months or less, under the supervision of some bankrupt tinker or illiterate dame that followed the double occupation of teaching and midwifery, and whom a distant dread of the poor-house drove from the land of his birth, and hear him contribute his share towards the defamation of the monks, and perhaps glory in the suppression of the monasteries, I pity that poor, old man.

Before closing this letter, I thought, I would see what the Methodist Watson, in his "Theological Dictionary," says about the Monks. Under "Monk" his offering can be found; it is well seasoned, and is ready for instant use—done up in mouthfuls for the preacher. According to him, the solitary life was proper enough during the early persecutions, when men, to escape death for their faith, had to seek secluded retreats; but he condemns them for continuing such a mode of life after the danger was past. Now, is it not barely possible, that those men would know how to shape their manner of life to their own times and circumstances, about as well as Mr. Watson? Though if they were driven hard they could allege for an excuse, that there were not any Methodist preachers, in those times, to give them sage counsel, and to fill them with wisdom and understanding. But Watson is no authority on these matters. His expression, "Capuchins and Franciscans," settles him down into his proper place. Some blotch of miserable ignorance generally disfigures the performances of such men.

LETTER V.

FRAGMENTS.

I intended to devote a letter to a subject, at the bare mention of which the Protestant swells with indignation —the Jesuits. But I forbear for two reasons: I shall have enough to say without it, and, to be plain, my historical knowledge of the Order is not what it ought to be. I know, though, from such men as Ranke, Macaulay, Parkman, and others, that as theologians, philosophers, scientists, explorers, educators, and missionaries, the Jesuits have always been in the front rank ; and, when we consider what forms of heresy they have headed off, doubled up, or choked to suffocation, and what doughty champions of the reform they have driven from corner to crack, we can easily understand how it is, that the teachers of Protestantism have not much to say in commendation of the Jesuits. But, if I have not read as much about them as I ought to have read, I have heard a good deal about them.

One evening when I was unconsciously working my way into the Church, I was called on by a clergyman. He was the master divine and ecclesiastical scholar of the neighborhood. He had had a regular training in college, could manage the Latin and the Greek to great satisfaction ; and, as he gave me to understand, was powerful in Hebrew. As soon as he came, I guessed the object of his visit. There was, I knew, a suspicion abroad, that I was wonderfully fascinated with Catholic reading ; and he had come to ascertain for himself the correctness of the report. A glance at my books confirmed his worst fears. His disapproval of my conduct was expressed by condemnatory shakes of the head, hard drawn sighs, and sundry ejaculations of contempt. After making a few common-place remarks, he opened out on the Jesuits. What he said I will not attempt to repeat ; but it would be speaking softly to call his utterances tirades. He spoke with all the decision of one who is thoroughly conversant with his subject. While he was having his own way with the distant enemy, he picked up, at a venture, DeMontor's "Lives of the Popes." As he became interested in looking at the portraits in the book, his rancor gradually abated. At last he came to a picture, and looking below it he drawled out, "Ig–na–tius Loy–o–la!" Turning his eyes to the headline of the opposite page, he saw PIUS VII.

"I suppose," said he, looking at me and pointing with his finger to Loyola, "this was PIUS VII., before he was Pope?"

"No," said I, "it is Ignatius Loyola."

"Oh, ah, yes, a Catholic of some kind, I dare say."

Whether this is with or without a point, it is strictly true; and somehow it begot in me the suspicion, that it is possible for a man, who has even "read the first twenty-five chapters of Genesis, in the original Hebrew," to be a little off in "Jesuitical" matters! In slander, though, the man was well up. But, for the particular benefit of such men, I will give a quotation from Mosheim, to show that it is possible to be too malignant, even in speaking of the Jesuits. "As this order has produced men of learning and genius, so neither has it been destitute of men of probity and candour; nor would it be a difficult task to compile from the writings of the Jesuits a much more just and proper representation of the duties of religion and the obligations of morality, than that hideous and unseemly exhibition of both, which Paschal and his followers have drawn from the Jesuitical Casuists, Summists, and Moralists. . . . The candour and impartiality that become an historian oblige us to acknowledge, at the same time, that in demonstrating the turpitude and enormity of certain maxims and opinions of the Jesuits, their adversaries have gone too far, and permitted their eloquence and zeal to run into exaggeration." (Vol. v. p. 196.)

This, drawn from such a partisan as Mosheim, should recall to a sense of common fairness all justly disposed men, before launching out into ruthless invective against an Order, which, for learning, intelligence, self-denial, zeal for the propagation of the Gospel, and the promotion of civilization, have no compeers, as their enemies admit ; but men of my clergyman's stamp will no doubt persevere in carrying on the usual campaign against a body of men, in which they would not, on grounds of scholastic qualifications, be accepted as simple postulants. When, however, men just as hardy, but better qualified, enter the lists against the Jesuits, they always find, that they have to contend with living men, who are fully competent to take care of themselves and to shake the conceit out of an unscrupulous adversary. Before passing from this subject, it was my intention to give a quotation from the English Waterton, the famous naturalist; and I do so, after much hesitation. It is so long. You can read it, or skip it. "Close by the riverside stands what is called the Palace of the Captain-General of Pernambuco. Its form and appearance altogether strike the traveler that it was never intended for the use it is at present put to.

"Reader, throw a veil over thy recollection for a little while, and forget the cruel, unjust, and unmerited censures thou hast heard against an unoffending order. This palace was once the Jesuits' college, and originally built by those charitable fathers. Ask the aged and respectable inhabitants of Pernambuco, and they will tell thee that the destruction of the Society of Jesus was a terrible disaster to the public, and its consequences severely felt to the present day.

"When Pombal took the reins of power into his own hands, virtue and learning beamed bright within the college walls. Public catechism to the children, and religious instruction to all, flowed daily from the mouths of its venerable priests.

"They were loved, revered, and respected throughout the whole town. The illuminating philosophers of the day had sworn to exterminate Christian knowledge, and the college of Pernambuco was doomed to founder in the general storm. To the long-lasting sorrow and disgrace of Portugal, the philosophers blinded her king and flattered her Prime Minister. Pombal was exactly the tool these sappers of every public and private virtue wanted. He had the naked sword of power in his own hand, and his heart was as hard as flint. He struck a mortal blow, and the Society of Jesus throughout the Portuguese dominions, was no more.

"One morning all the fathers of the college in Pernambuco, some of them very old and feeble, were suddenly ordered into the refectory. They had notice beforehand of the fatal storm, in pity from the governor, but not one of them abandoned his charge. They had done their duty, and had nothing to fear. They bowed with resignation to the will of Heaven. As soon as they had all reached the refectory, they were there locked up, and never more did they see their rooms, their friends, their scholars, or acquaintance. In the dead of the following night, a strong guard of soldiers literally drove them through the streets to the water's edge. They were then conveyed in boats aboard a ship, and steered for Bahia. Those who survived the barbarous treatment they experienced from Pombal's creatures were at last ordered to Lisbon. The college of Pernambuco was plundered, and some time after an elephant was kept there.

"Thus the arbitrary hand of power, in one night, smote and swept away the sciences; to which succeeded the low vulgar buffoonery of a showman. Virgil and Cicero made way for a wild beast from Angola! and now a guard is on duty at the very gate where, in times long past, the poor were daily fed!!!

"Trust not, kind reader, to the envious remarks which their enemies have scattered far and near; believe not the stories of those who have had a hand in the sad tragedy. Go to Brazil, and see with thine own eyes the effect of Pombal's short-sighted policy. There vice reigns triumphant, and learning is at its lowest ebb. Neither is this to be wondered at. Destroy the compass, and will the vessel find her far-distant port? Will the flock keep together, and escape the wolves, after the shepherds are all slain? The Brazilians were told that public education would go on just as usual. They might have asked Government, who so able to instruct our youth as those whose knowledge is proverbial? who so fit as those who enjoy our entire confidence? who so worthy, as those whose lives are irreproachable?

"They soon found that those who succeeded the fathers of the Society of Jesus had neither their manner nor their abilities. They had not made the instruction of youth their particular study. Moreover, they entered on the field after a defeat, where the officers had all been slain: where the plan of the campaign was lost; where all was in sorrow and dismay. No exertions of theirs could rally the dispersed, or skill prevent the fatal consequences. At the present day the seminary of Olinda, in comparison with the former Jesuits' college, is only as the waning moon's beam to the sun's meridian splendour.

"When you visit the places where those learned fathers once flourished, and see with your own eyes the evils their dissolution has caused: when you hear the inhabitants telling you how good, how clever, how charitable they were—what will you think of our poet laureate for calling them, in his 'History of Brazil,' 'Missioners, whose zeal the most fanatical was directed by the coolest policy'?

"Was it *fanatical* to renounce the honours and comforts of this transitory life, in order to gain eternal glory in the next, by denying themselves, and taking up the cross? Was it *fanatical* to preach salvation to innumerable wild hordes of Americans, to clothe the naked, to encourage the repenting sinner, to aid the dying Christian? The fathers of the Society of Jesus did all this. And for this their zeal is pronounced to be the most fanatical, directed by the coolest policy. It will puzzle many a clear brain to comprehend how it is possible, in the nature of things, that *zeal* the most *fanatical* should be directed by the *coolest policy*. Ah, Mr. Laureate, Mr. Laureate, that ' quidlibet audendi' of yours may now and then gild the poet, at the same time that it makes the historian cut a sorry figure.

"Could Father Nobrega rise from the tomb, he would thus address you :—' Ungrateful Englishman, you have drawn a great part of your information from the writings of the Society of Jesus, and in return you attempt to stain its character by telling your country-men that "we taught the idolatry we believed !" In speaking of me, you say, it was my happy fortune to be stationed in a country where *none* but the good principles of my order were called into action. Ungenerous laureate, the narrow policy of the times has kept your countrymen in the dark with regard to the true character of the Society of Jesus; and you draw the bandage still tighter over their eyes by a malicious insinuation. I lived, and taught, and died in Brazil, where you state that *none* but the good principles of my order were called into action, and still, in most absolute contradiction to this, you remark we believed the *idolatry* we taught in Brazil. Thus we brought none but good principles into action, and still taught idolatry !

"'Again, you state there is no individual to whose talents Brazil is so greatly and permanently indebted as mine, and that I must be regarded as the founder of that system so successfully pursued by the Jesuits in Paraguay : a system productive of as much good as is compatible with pious fraud. Thus you make me, at one and the same time, a teacher of none but good principles, and a teacher of idolatry, and a believer in idolatry, and still the founder of a system for which Brazil is greatly and permanently indebted to me, though, by-the-bye, the system was only productive of as much good as is compatible with pious fraud!

"'What means all this? After reading such incomparable nonsense, should your countrymen wish to be properly informed concerning the Society of Jesus, there are in England documents enough to show that the system of the Jesuits was a system of Christian charity towards their fellow-creatures, administered in a manner which human prudence judged best calculated to ensure success; and that the idolatry which you uncharitably affirm they taught was really and truly the very same faith which the Catholic Church taught for centuries in England, which she still teaches to those who wish to hear her, and which she will continue to teach pure and unspotted, till time shall be no more.'" ("Wanderings in South America," Second Journey.)

Perhaps nothing keeps up the steady aversion of Protestants from Catholicity, more than those oft repeated miscellaneous charges against the Church, which were at first nothing except gratuitous assertions, but seemingly expected to be battered into truth, by bold and frequent repetition. Each and every one of them has been refuted time and again; but, through interest or ignorance, they are often rehabilitated in all their old factitious garbs.

Almost every Protestant, for instance, is sure, that, before Martin Luther lived, no one knew anything of the Bible. The world is indebted to Martin for its general distribution, at least. But how did Martin find out that such a book was in existence? Any common Protestant historian will tell us. Here is the "Life of Luther," by Martyn, published by the American Tract Society. On page 38, he says: "One day —he (Luther) was then in his twentieth year, and had been at the university two years—while engaged as usual in glancing over the library manuscripts, he chanced to open an old volume, mouldy and cobwebbed. Attracted by its antique aspect, Luther read its title, and found it to be *a Latin Bible*, the first he had ever seen. This he read and reread with inexpressible and never-ceasing delight, mingled with some astonishment, for until then he had imagined that the fragments of Scripture contained in the various collects of the Roman ritual embraced the whole word of God." This is the way it is generally put; and, of course, that, but for this providential discovery, we should now know nothing of the Bible. The story carries an absurdity on its very face; and its utter falsity is easily demonstrated. Editions upon editions of the whole Bible, both in Latin and in several vernaculars, had been printed and circulated, before Luther was born; and who will believe that Luther had not seen some of them. "Before the year 1200, the English had translated into their own dialect, in prose, the Psalter and the Canticles of the Church; and towards the middle of the thirteenth century they seem to have possessed a prose version of the entire Bible." (Hardwick's M. A. p. 297.)   "The old High-German version, printed first at Mentz, 1462, was reprinted *ten* times before the Reformation. In like manner an Italian version, printed at Venice as early as 1471, is said to have gone through *nine* editions in the fifteenth century." (Id. p. 360.)   "In 1478 there appeared from the same press (Valencia) a translation of the Scriptures, in the Limousin, by Father Boniface Ferrer, brother of the famous Dominican, St. Vincent Ferrer."(Prescott's " Ferdinand and Isabella," Vol. I. p. 387.)   "As the various languages of Europe became gradually developed, a desire naturally arose amongst those who spoke them for services in the vernacular; and this desire was not left altogether ungratified even long before the Reformation. Thus, in England, the Epistles and Gospels and the Litany were translated into the native language in the Services of the Church, and interlinear translations were made of many portions of the Mediæval Prayer Books. Neither must we imagine that the translations of Holy Scripture put forth by the Reformers, or even that earlier version to which Wickliffe gave his name, were by any means the first efforts made to produce the Holy Bible in the vernacular. From Anglo-Saxon times downwards, we have traces of Bibles translated for the use of those who preferred such versions; and to the truth of this statement may be quoted the testimony of John Foxe, the "martyrologist," who says, 'If histories be well examined, we shall find, both before the Conquest and after, as well before John Wickliffe was born as since, the whole body of the Scriptures by sundry men translated into this our country tongue.'" (Blunt's Key to Ch. Hist., p. 117.) "Thus it was that the Apocryphal Epistle (to the Laodiceans) passed into the early vernacular translations of the New Testament. It is said that fourteen editions of one or more German versions were printed before Luther's time; and it occurs in the first Bohemian Bible (1488)." (Westcott's "Canon of the New Testament," p. 461.) The same story of Luther's finding the Bible, is told by Milner in his Church History, and Dr. Maitland, in referring to it, says: "Really one hardly knows how to meet such statements, . . To say nothing of *parts* of the Bible, or of books whose *place* is uncertain, we know of at least *twenty* different *editions* of the *whole* Latin Bible *printed* in *Germany* only before Luther was *born*. These had issued from Augsburg, Strasburg, Cologne, Ulm, Mentz (two), Basil (four), Nuremberg (ten), and were dispersed through Germany, I repeat, before Luther was born; and I may add that before that event there was a printing press at work in this very town of Erfurt, where, more than twenty years after, he is said to have made his 'discovery.' . . No doubt we should be within the truth if we were to say that beside the multitude of manuscript copies, not yet fallen into disuse, the *press* had issued fifty different editions of the whole Latin Bible; to say nothing of Psalters, New Testaments, or other parts.

And yet, more than twenty years after, we find a young man who had received 'a very liberal education,' who 'had made great proficiency in his studies at Magdeburg, Eisenach, and Erfurt,' and who, nevertheless, did not know what a Bible was, simply because 'the Bible was unknown in those days.'" (D. A., p. 469.)

Who does not know that the Catholics have entirely suppressed one of the commandments, and, to still have ten, have split one of the remaining nine into two parts? Watson, in his Theol. Dict., gives a detailed account of the abominable trick. But let any one, after reading Watson's, or any similar account, procure a Catholic catechism and examine it, to decide for himself who is guilty of what is worse than the lowest kind of trickery. The Catholics do not suppress an iota of the commandments. Concerning the division, Blunt, in his "Key to the Catechism," puts the matter fairer: "The commandments are numbered as ten in all by God Himself. But the exact mode of division is not declared in the Bible. The Continental Churches and the Lutherans divide our first into the first and second, and unite our ninth and tenth into one. This division is very ancient, but our own seems to be most correctly in agreement with the exact number." (p. 113.) The bare thought of this "suppression" and "division" stirs up the temper of the aspiring exhorter pretty badly sometimes. If he cannot have the ten commandments, entire and properly divided, what is there left for him? Well, as far as the commandments go, it is to be feared, that, without the Book, he and his like would not have much left; because I believe, that, if one half of the preachers (I except the Anglicans and the Presbyterians) were suddenly called on to repeat in order the ten commandments, their failure would be as signal as disgraceful. Besides, do they in or out of their Sunday Schools trouble themselves about teaching the commandments to their children? They do nothing of the sort.

All their pretentious concern about the commandments goes for nothing but superfluous twaddle. If they value them at all, they would teach them to the young.

Then again, for hundreds and hundreds of years prior to the "Reformation," "nothing was done towards giving the people scriptural instruction." In those times the clergy were sordid and depraved: the people were unreflecting devotees of the most revolting superstitions. Dr. Maitland gives, most certainly, a faithful draught of the opinion held by many concerning those times. He says: "I believe that the idea which many persons have of ecclesiastical history may be briefly stated thus: that the Christian church was a small, scattered, and persecuted flock, until the time of Constantine; that then, at once, and as if by magic, the Roman world became Christian; that this Universal Christianity, not being of a very pure, solid, or durable nature, melted down into a filthy mass called Popery, which held its place during the dark ages, until the revival of Pagan literature, and the consequent march of intellect, sharpened men's wits and brought about the Reformation; when it was discovered that the pope was Antichrist, and that the saints had been in the hands of the little horn predicted by the prophet Daniel for hundreds of years without knowing so awful a fact, or suspecting anything of the kind." (D. A. p. 188.) Is there any history to justify this vulgar opinion? Without question there is sufficient of what purports to be history to make it all good, which is well known to the readers of Mosheim and of those who have made his work the first source of their information the Robertsons, the Whites, the Milners, etc. Whatever Mosheim presented has been taken in and thrown out for the gospel truth. It has, however, lately been discovered that Mosheim, his translator, if not his slavish imitators, have deliberately falsified history, in order to cast a shade upon the Church. "The 'Ecclesiastical History' he wrote," says the Protestant Baring-Gould, "is full of perversions of the plainest facts, and that under our notice is but one out of many. . This is but of a piece with his malignity and disregard for truth, whenever he can hit the Catholic Church hard." ("Mediæval Myths," p. 106.) And Baring-Gould is right. Who knows not, for instance, of the mutilated extracts which he crushed together, and which "the learned and judicious" Maclaine so sweetly summarized, for a homily of St. Eligius, Bishop of Noyon ? In connection with this, Waddington, who seems to have felt a little piqued, when he "ascertained the treachery of his historical conductor (Mosheim)," concluded his remarks on the subject with this : "If the very essence of history be truth, and if any deliberate violation of that be sinful in the profane annalist, still less can it deserve pardon or mercy in the historian of the Church of Christ." (Ch. Hist. p. 252.) And Hallam says : "But it is due to justice that this extract from Eligius should never be quoted in future, as the translator of Mosheim has induced Robertson and many others, as well as myself, to do." ("Middle Ages," p. 606.) Maitland, "Dark Ages," pp. 100—122, gives a full and ingenious exposure of it. I advise you to get and read Maitland's work. The book is hard to get, I well know, but, if you find it impossible to get a copy, do all you can to induce some of the Tract Societies to reissue it. If you care to know anything about old times, the book will certainly please you. On page 33, he gives an idea about the past, that you will certainly indorse, if you give it any thought. "I cannot tell why, in things pertaining to the kingdom of God, and on which man can be enlightened only by the word and Spirit of God, they might not be as truly, and even as fully, enlightened as any of mankind before or after their time." And this opinion has the confirmation of history. Speaking of the ninth century, Hardwick says : "Many of the councils have, however, laid especial stress on the necessity of preaching in the native dialects. They urge that opportunity should be afforded, both in town and country parishes, of gaining a complete acquaintance with the precious Word of God. The doctrines of the Saviour's incarnation, death, and final triumph in behalf of man, the gift of the Holy Ghost, the value of the sacraments, the blessedness of joining in the act of public prayer, the need of pure and upright living, and the certainty of future judgment in accordance with men's works, are recommended as the leading topics for the expositions of the priest." ("Middle Ages," p. 192.) On page 310, he says: "But on the other hand we should remember that anomalies which differ only in degree present themselves in every age of Christianity, nay, more or less, in every human heart; and that in spite of very much to sadden and perplex us in our study of the Middle Age, there is enough in men like Anselm, Bernard, Louis IX. of France, Aquinas, Grosseteste, and if we include the gentler sex, Elizabeth of Hessen, Hedwige of Poland, and a host of others, to attest the permanent influence of Christian truth and real saintliness of life." On page 44, he says: "The Benedictines and their offshoots were peculiarly devoted to the study of the Bible." "There are also good grounds for believing that the provision made by the Church for the spiritual necessities of the people was not, at any rate, less abundant than is the case at the present day. Indeed, there is no doubt that both Churches and Clergy, and consequently opportunities for worship and instruction, were far more in proportion to the number and needs of the population than they can be said to be now in our own country, even after the persevering and liberal efforts of late years." (Blunt's Key to Ch. Hist. p. 116.)

The prominent "reformers" and troops of their followers used to lay it down as an incontrovertible truth, that the Pope is Antichrist (St. Matt. x. 25); and the obscure, country preacher, and very often the baffled disputant, even now-a-days, solemnly declare the same thing. Their counterfeit sincerity must be the apology for their malignity; but the blasphemous statement is readily believed by the people. They ought to know, though, that to-day it is not fashionable, at least, to say so. "It is disputed by many of our theologians, whether those prophecies really relate to the Roman pontiffs: but supposing that they do, I deny absolutely the conclusion which is attempted to be drawn from them, for all who apply these prophecies to the Roman see affirm, that the reign of Antichrist had begun, at latest, in the eighth century; but the universal church of Christ held communion with the see of Rome till the eleventh century at least; therefore, according to this objection, the whole church of Christ must have failed and become apostate for several centuries, which is a decidedly heretical position, contrary to the Christian faith. Therefore we may assume it as certain, that communion with the Roman see is no sign of apostacy from Christ." (Palmer's "Church," Vol. 1. p. 309.) Dr. Schaff, Professor of Church History in the Union Theological Seminary at New York, in his "Creed Revision," page 33, says: "Finally, we venture to raise an objection which has not been touched at all in this discussion, as far as I have seen, .. but which I feel very strongly, both on moral as well as exegetical and historical grounds. I will mention it at the risk of provoking the opposition of many Presbyterian friends whom I highly esteem. It is the declaration of the Confession that the Pope (p. 34) of Rome is the Antichrist, and that Papists, that is, all Roman Catholics, are idolaters. I protest against this judgment as untrue, unjust, unwise, uncharitable, and unsuitable in any Confession of Faith. It is a colossal slander on the oldest and largest Church of Christendom. . . . . The Pope of Rome is the legitimate head of the Roman Church, and as such he has the same rights and privileges as the Eastern Patriarchs or the Archbishops of Canterbury and York have over their respective dioceses. He is older than any one of them, and his line goes back in unbroken succession to Clement of Rome at the end of the first century... (p. 35).. The alleged proof-text in 2 Thess. ii. 3, 4, refers to 'the mystery of lawlessness' (not 'iniquity,' as the Authorized Version has it), which was 'at work already' (verse 7) in the time of Paul, before there was any popery. If he had had popery in mind, he would have warned against it in the Epistle to the Romans, and not in that to the Thessalonians... As to the term 'antichrist,' it only occurs in the Epistles of John (1 John ii. 18, 22; iv. 3; 2 John 7), and is used not of a future individual, but of contemporaries of the Apostle, of heretical teachers in Asia Minor, who had been members of the Church, and left it, and who denied the incarnation and the real humanity of Christ. The pope has never done this, but, on the contrary, has ever held those doctrines with the utmost tenacity, and can never give them up... It seems incredible that a body of intelligent and well-educated Christian ministers, as the majority of Presbyterians undoubtedly are, should be able to entertain such a monstrous proposition." "It is a strange instance of religionary virulence which makes some detect the Pope of Rome in the Man of Sin, the Harlot, the Beast,.. There is nothing Roman in this, but something very much the opposite. How the Abomination of Desolation can be considered as set up in a Church where every sanctuary is adorned with all that can draw the heart to the Crucified, and raise the thoughts to the imposing ritual of Heaven, is a puzzle to me. To a man uninitiated in the law that Revelation is to be interpreted by contraries, it would seem more like the Abomination of Desolation in the Holy Place if he entered a Scotch Presbyterian, or a Dutch Calvinist, place of worship. Rome does not fight against the Daily Sacrifice, and endeavor to abolish it ; that has been rather the labor of so-called Church Reformers, who with the suppression of the doctrine of Eucharistic Sacrifice and Sacramental Adoration have well nigh obliterated all notion of worship to be addressed to the God-Man. Rome does not deny the power of the godliness of which she makes show, but insists on that power with no broken accents. It is rather in other communities, where authority is flung aside, and any man is permitted to believe or reject what he likes, that we must look for the leaven of the Anti-christian spirit at work." (Baring-Gould's "Mediæval Myths," p. 97.)

If this anti-Christ theory has any basis whatever, it must be fatal to Protestantism itself, provided that an uncorrupted text of the Sacred Scriptures be necessary for the new religion. According to some Protestant explorers, the origin of the anti-christian power plays between A. D. 200, and A. D. 500. Taking the latter mark, we have, from A. D. 500 to A. D. 1500, Luther's time, a good, round, one thousand years. For one thousand years, then, anti-Christ lived in Rome, and ruled what has been improperly called Christendom. But it is past all dispute, that the Man in Rome and his Council have been the custodians and conveyancers to us, of the Holy Scriptures. Anti-Christ had unrestricted control of the Bible, for one thousand years. Now, let me ask, with what semblance of propriety can the Pope be called anti-Christ, unless he did his utmost to turn the books that show forth Christ, into nonsensical fables or false narratives? What other work could he do, to maintain his character? If the anti-Christ theory be true, the Bible will hardly be the Word of God ; if it is the Word of God, the Pope is not Anti-Christ. If the Protestants wish to exalt the authority of the Bible, they should speak truthfully and reverently of the Catholic Church from which they took it.

The occasional declaration that Catholics are allowed,

or encouraged, to violate "promises made to heretics," when their interests are bettered by doing so, is another calumny that the "evangelicals" will no doubt continue to repeat. I understand, though, that something of the kind was once put forth by the Geneva party. Collier says, that, in the Geneva translation of the Bible, the marginal comment on St. Matt. II. 12, contains these: "that promise ought not to be kept where God's honour and preaching of his truth is hindered, or else it ought not to be broken." (Vol. VII. p. 292.)

The time was when I looked upon that story in Mosheim, about the management of a half-wit called Tetzer, by some Dominicans, as a sample instance of the low cunning practised by Catholics, to delude a credulous people. As it stands, it rests solely on Protestant authority; and I think, that, when Burnet is used to substantiate it, one might be pardoned for laughing at the whole thing. But even if it were true, it can be matched. In Collier's History, you can find this: "About this time some of the reformed were remarkably ungoverned in their zeal. For instance: there was a cat hung upon a gallows in Cheapside, and something of the habit of a priest put upon her. This figure was carried to the bishop of London, and shown in the pulpit at Paul's cross by Dr. Pendilton. Not long after, a pistol was discharged at this Pendilton, in the same place. The bullet drove into the church wall, and missed him very narrowly. To these disorders I shall subjoin another which looked like a deeper contrivance. For the purpose: one Elizabeth Crofts had been practised with to set up an imposture; she delivered very offensive discourse through a wall near Aldersgate in London. The matter was so artificially managed, that the voice was heard, but no person discovered. This 'spirit in the wall,' as it was called, was cried up for a most miraculous intelligence from the other world. Some said it was an angel, and others made it no less than the immediate warning of the Holy Ghost. The sound was conveyed by a whistle given her for that purpose by one Drake, servant to Sir Anthony Nevil. She had several assistants to carry on the cheat. These confederates, mixing with the crowd, undertook to expound the spirit, and delivered the oracle in seditious language against the queen and the prince of Spain, and declaimed strongly against the mass, against confession, and such other doctrines of the anti-reformed. All this was confessed by the maid herself upon a scaffold at Paul's Cross. . . . These, it must be owned, were very unjustifiable sallies. What could be more provoking to the court, than to see the queen's (Mary's) honour aspersed, their religion insulted, their preachers shot at in the pulpit, and a lewd imposture played against the government? Had the reformed been more smooth and inoffensive in their behaviour, had the eminent clergy of that party published an abhorrence of such unwarrantable methods, it is possible, some may say, they might have met with gentler usage, and prevented the persecution from flaming out." (Vol. VI. p. 83.)

I will close this letter with a few extracts:—

"The authority of the priests operated in the darker ages as a salutary antidote: they prevented the total extinction of letters, mitigated the fierceness of the times, sheltered the poor and defenceless, and preserved or revived the peace and order of civil society." (Gibbon's Hist., Vol. VI. p. 131.)

"It goes to show that, at the darkest periods, the Christian Church was the source and spring of civilization, the dispenser of what little comfort and security there was in the things of this world, and the quiet scriptural assertor of the rights of man." (Maitland's D. A, p. 393.)

"Perhaps no feature of the Middle Ages is more striking than the influence of the Church in teaching the equality of men, and opening a way to preferment for the humblest of her members. Any one might be received into a monastery: he could then be ordained, and if possessing superior qualifications might advance to the very highest eminence in Church and State. In this manner some of the evils, arising out of the hereditary character of feudalism, were largely counteracted; and the Church became the champion and promoter of popular rights." (Hardwick's Mid. Ages, p. 55.)

"It cannot, however, be denied that the Church employed its influence to restrain it (slavery); the clergy in general, and especially several Popes, enforced the manumission of their slaves as a duty incumbent upon laymen, and loudly inveighed against the scandal of keeping Christians in bondage." (Guizot's Hist. of Civilization, p. 112.) On page 115, he says: "She (Church) endeavoured by every means in her power to suppress the frequent recourse which at this period was had to violence and the continual wars to which society was so prone. It is well known what the truce of God was, as well as a number of other similar measures by which the Church hoped to prevent the employment of physical force, and to introduce into the social system more order and gentleness."

"The hierarchy, addressing itself to the religious spirit, but in a manner conformed to the age, endeavoured to establish the ascendancy of the law and of an elevated morality. A period in which brute force was the only law, was interrupted by one in which the *Truce of God* was sustained by ecclesiastical threatenings and miracles. Women and children, defenceless persons, and every thing constructed or planted for purposes of peace, were in times of war under the protection of the Church." (Hase's Ch. Hist., p. 219.) A saying of the Middle Ages was, "*It is good to live under the crook.*"

LETTER VI.

TEMPORAL POWER OF THE POPES.

Amongst Protestants, as there always have been among heretics, there are a few men who have a weakness to be called Catholics: they are the highest grade of the outsiders, who know some of the glories of Catholicity, and are consumed with a desire to be regarded as actual members of it. They love the name, they put it on exhibition, and they dance around it; but they have an insuperable objection against embracing the reality. Their great bugbear is the Papacy. Only for that they would soon be happy! For the other Protestants, "the sects," they have a lordly contempt, and "the sects" have a healthy hatred of them; but, when they touch the subject of "Papalism," and lay bare "the usurpations" and "the tyrannical acts" of the Gregorys and the Innocents, and call on "the sects" for a general chorus of "Papal tyranny," then "Papal tyranny" becomes the undersong of a reconciled family. And, although their union with the despised "sects" is formed only to be as quickly dissolved, they will any time sink all differences, to re-unite for a common onslaught. For a long time this curious fact had a restraining effect upon me. The conduct of "the sects" affected me in no way, for I have never supposed that their acquaintance with the Papacy is either intimate or profound; but I had credited the "Catholics" with having a detailed knowledge of papal affairs, and I thought, that, when they, who must so well understand the whole matter, so far lower their standards as to fraternize with the "sects," they make a praiseworthy sacrifice of feeling and principles in the interests of civil freedom. For, if the

Papacy be the sole objection to their adoption of Catholicity, it must be as abominable as Protestants have represented it. In short, it held me for a long time to the opinion, that the Papacy, and especially that phase of it called the Temporal Power, has been in its origin and exercise something that should be reprobated by every man who is inspired with a love for civil liberty.

Nor was I altogether without particular proofs for my anti-papal position. Where it was I can not say now, but some where I once saw a picture in which a pope had his foot upon the neck of a prostrate man, an emperor. It was Alexander III. and Barbarossa. To me it was for a long time a sample instance of papal haughtiness. In the arrogant and bitter look of the Pope there was enough to create in any one an abiding hatred of all Popes. The picture, without words, expressed enough. Now, any thing offered as an historical fact, and illustrated with a woodcut, ought to be true. But I was disgusted to find out, when reading Milman's "Latin Christianity," that the whole affair is what delicate people call a figment. Milman says: "Such a fiction is extraordinary. . . . As Poetry has often become, here Painting for once became History." (See Vol. IV. p. 435.) Can it be possible, I thought, that all those terrible stories, so derogatory to the Papacy, will also be found upon examination to have been constructed for effect or to have originated in hatred? I can not stay to specify them; but I soon satisfied myself, that the weightiest of them were originally without the slightest foundation on fact; and whoever will take the trouble to discover their origin and trace their growth, will come to the conclusion, that they are more disgraceful to their retailers than to the Popes. Again I found myself confronting a new task, an examination of the Papacy, as regards temporal matters. Have I mastered the history of the Papacy? I have studied enough about it to know better than to make any such ridiculous pretension; but enough, I believe, to know that the ordinary declaimer against "Papal usurpations" and "Papal tyranny" is a man that generally charges a very low fee for his show.

There is nothing in history that deserves a more careful and dispassionate study than the history of the Papacy; nor is there any other historical subject that will require so much time, patience, or assiduous application. When we bear in mind, that, during the first three centuries, the external organization of the Church was frequently broken up, or apparently crushed, by the attacks of Paganism, that most of the Popes were martyrs for the faith, and that all Christians lived in expectation of a speedy death, there should be no marvel that the history of the period may seem to be somewhat fragmentary or obscure. The wonder should be, that the accounts of the virtues and sufferings of every Pope that ruled throughout the period, were chronicled and have been preserved for us. But several writers flourished within that time, and, if they did not accumulate the particulars with which a consecutive and full history of ecclesiastical matters might be constructed, they have provided sufficient to show, that, although the Church was fiercely assailed, she was steadily expanding her sphere and enclosing in her fold multiplying numbers; and that nothing apparently contributed as much to her progress, nothing so much attracted converts or recommended her to the respect of her enemies, as the mortified lives, the self-denying labors, and the eminent virtues, of the clergy. The sterling characters of the bishops contrasted so sharply with the profligate lives of the Flamens, that in authority and influence the former were steadily, if slowly, gaining the ascendant. Like all other ancient nations, the Romans regarded religion as an invaluable aid to the government, in fostering in the people a respect for the law, and inculcating the maxims of morality; and naturally enough, from the beneficial nature of their functions, the ministers of religion were held in high consideration, and accorded a high standing in the State. They received ample revenues, and were exempt from municipal and other civil duties and obligations; and so extensive were the power and privileges of the sovereign Flamen, that it is hard to discover in what respect he was inferior to the highest civil magistrate. But all their authority and emoluments were to be transferred to the clergy of the Christian religion. The conversion of Constantine was the turning point in the change.

As the Roman laws peremptorily forbade the introduction or the practice of a new religion, the Church, although in the State, had been considered and treated by the Emperors as an alien to the State. She had been an outlaw, and as an institution had had no legal rights. But Constantine shortly after his conversion, in conjunction with Licinius, passed the Edict of Milan, A. D. 313, which gave the Christian religion full toleration and a legal status; so that what property the Church had held before by sufferance, she could henceforth hold by law. Constantine also conferred upon the clergy special tokens of his confidence and esteem; and, by granting that cases of appeal from secular judges might be referred to the arbitration of Bishops for a definitive sentence, he raised to commanding influence the Episcopal order. But, as the bishops were raised to authority, the Pope, the Bishop of bishops, was raised with them, and above them. To these pledges of his respect and reverence for the Christian clergy, he added several munificent donations and settled grants, that placed them in a position of worldly respectability, which, among people such as the Romans were, greatly enhanced in popular estimation the religion of which they were the professors and teachers. Against all this two objections have been strongly urged: that temporal power is incompatible with spiritual power, and that the ministers of religion are disqualified from holding property. The first objection is easily confuted by Scriptural examples. Both temporal and spiritual power were exercised by Moses and by the holiest characters of the Old Testament times; and they all derived their powers from the institution of the Almighty. And where in the New Testament are the ministers of Christ forbidden to wield temporal power? Where has He declared, that they are or must be incapacitated for the duties of intelligent and useful, civil rulers? Do the notions of morality, justice, and humanity, which they learned from Him, disqualify them? The second objection is paltrier still; as it cannot be sustained by any thing, positive or inferential, from Scripture.

The motives that prevailed with Constantine to bestow such lavish endowments on the Church and to make the clergy administrators of civil affairs, are neither deep nor hidden. He well knew with what a high sense of justice the clergy were imbued; with what satisfaction their impartial decisions had been received, when their jurisdiction had been limited to deciding the differences of Christians, before the Church had had Imperial recognition; and that their disengagement from the world would be a good guarantee that they would be proof against the seductions of bribery. But a motive no less probable is, that, having detected the germs of dissolution that had even then taken deep root in the heart of the Empire, he saw in a firmly erected Christian Church a powerful and efficient agent for making moral and loyal subjects, and so a prop and stay to the State.

On a superficial view it may seem that Constantine's confidence was sadly misplaced, since the Church was powerless to prevent the downfall of the Empire. But Constantine himself broke it up by partitioning it among his sons; and, if the Church did not then save it, she eased its fall. It should be borne in mind, though, that after Constantine's death she was beset with difficulties that greatly embarrassed her concerted action. Arianism, the Paganism of Julian, and the jealous, not to say vicious, intermeddling with dogmatic questions, by successive emperors, were disheartening hindrances to the propagation of true Christianity. When the saints were in exile, how could the common clergy, harassed and thwarted, pursue prosperous courses? But it was during these very times, that, by enfranchising slaves, redeeming captives, erecting hospitals, instituting the right of sanctuary, relieving the poor, and exhibiting in the persons of their greatest confessors a sturdy zeal for truth and principle, the clergy secured the gratitude and admiration of a despondent people. And in the clergy they found their only protectors. Pope Leo turned back from Rome the barbarians, Attila and Genseric; Pope Zachary saved Rome from the ruthless swords of Liutprand and Rachis.

Now, what could be more natural than a gradual increase of the Pope's temporal power? Beginning with an authority derived through Constantine, constitutionally enlarged by Honorius and other emperors, and increased at the pressing requests of the people who sheltered themselves under its beneficent protection, it appeared in Gregory the Great almost equal to independent sovereignty. And Milman will tell us whether it was the fruit of long calculating ambition or not. "In the person of Gregory the Bishop of Rome first became, in act and in influence, if not in avowed authority, a temporal sovereign. Nor were his acts the ambitious encroachments of ecclesiastical usurpation on the civil power. They were forced upon him by the purest motives, if not by absolute necessity. The virtual sovereignty fell to him as abdicated by the neglect or powerlessness of its rightful owners: he must assume it, or leave the city and the people to anarchy. He alone could protect Rome and the remnant of her citizens from barbaric servitude; his authority rested on the universal feeling of its beneficence; his title was the security afforded by his government." (L. C. Vol. II. p. 73.) "The merits of Gregory were treated by the Byzantine court with reproach and insult; but in the attachment of a grateful people, he found the purest reward of a citizen, and the best right of a sovereign." (Gibbon's Hist., Vol. IV. p. 425.) "Until the time of *Gregory*, the papacy contended for dominion over the Church, not so much because the popes themselves were ambitious to acquire it, as because the necessities of the times and of those who understood them compelled them to do so." (Hase's Ch. Hist., p. 183.) Milman, after enumerating other causes that may have aided in consolidating the papal power, says (L. C., Vol. IV. p. 466.) "But after all, none of these accessory and, in some degree, fortuitous aids could have raised the Papal authority to its commanding height, had it not possessed more sublime and more lawful (!) claims to the reverence of mankind. It was still an assertion of eternal principles of justice, righteousness, and humanity."

And, to him who has never been able to see any thing but the "Decretals" for the foundation of the Papal authority, I offer these three extracts for careful consideration. "And it must be conceded that the spurious decretals contain very little which had not been actually asserted by some pope at one time or another." (Hase's Ch. Hist., p. 185.) "It is even now asserted, perhaps can hardly be disproved, that the False Decretals advanced no pretensions in favor of the See of Rome which had not been heard before in some vague and indefinite, but not therefore less significant, language." (Milman's L. C., Vol. III. p. 63.) "As if a piece of paper or parchment, especially in times when most people were unable to read, when the sword was in higher estimation than the pen, would have been able to erect a despotism, to which all bowed." (Hergenrother's "Anti-Janus," p. 223.)

Milman (Vol. ii. p. 42.) says too: "Now was the crisis in which the Papacy must re-awaken its obscured and suspended life. It was the only power which lay not entirely and absolutely prostrate before the disasters of the times—a power which had an inherent strength, and might resume its majesty. It was this power which was most imperatively required to preserve all which was to survive out of the crumbling wreck of Roman civilization. To Western Christianity was absolutely necessary a centre, standing alone, strong in traditionary reverence, and in acknowledged claims to supremacy. Even the perfect organization of the Christian hierarchy might in all human probability have fallen to pieces in perpetual conflict: it might have degenerated into a half secular feudal caste with hereditary benefices, more and more entirely subservient to the civil authority, a priesthood of each nation or each tribe, gradually sinking to the intellectual or religious level of the nation or tribe. On the rise of a power both controlling and conservative, hung, humanly speaking, the life and death of Christianity—of Christianity as a permanent, aggressive, expansive, and, to a certain extent, uniform system There must be a counterbalance to barbaric force, to the unavoidable anarchy of Teutonism. with its tribal, or at the utmost national independence, forming a host of small, conflicting, antagonistic kingdoms. All Europe would have been what England was under the Octarchy, what Germany was when her emperors were weak; and even her emperors she owed to Rome, to the Church, to Christianity. Providence might have otherwise ordained, but it is impossible for man to imagine by what other organizing or consolidating force the commonwealth of the Western nations could have grown up to a discordant, indeed, and conflicting league, but still to a league, with that unity and conformity of manners, usages, laws, religion, which have made their rivalries, oppugnancies, and even their long ceaseless wars, on the whole to issue in the noblest, highest, most intellectual form of civilization known to man."

From the time of Gregory the Great to Gregory III., the Popes were the defenders of Rome and many other Italian cities, against the unceasing attacks of the Lombards. In all their measures for the general safety, they were cheerfully obeyed by the citizens. During the pontificate of Gregory III., Luitprand laid close seige to Rome: the city was reduced to the last extremity. Leo the Isaurian would not or could not come to its relief. The Pope implored aid from Charles Martel. No other course was open. Abandoned to fate by the Emperor, the Pope, to avert the destruction of the city and to save his people from slavery or death, called the French into Italy. Martel's immediate outset for Rome was prevented by his sudden death. Pope Zachary, the successor of Gregory, not only managed to tranquilize Italy for a time, but prevailed on the Lombard to restore to the Holy See several cities that he had taken from it. After the death of Pope Zachary, the Lombard king Astolphus besieged Rome in regular form. The new Pope, Stephen II, arrested the progress of the siege by negotiation; but, discovering that the perfidious Lombard paid no respect to treaties, he went to France to seek the aid of Pepin. The French king, at the head of a well appointed army, went into Italy, inflicted on the Lombards a crushing defeat, and compelled Astolphus to swear that he would restore to the Pope what he had wrested from him. No sooner had the French turned their backs on Italy than Astolphus recommenced hostilities. Again Pepin entered Italy and compelled Astolphus to fulfill still harder conditions: he forced him to grant by a formal deed all the territories and cities of which the Holy See had been plundered. Renewed aggressions of the Lombards forced Pope Adrian to beseech the succor of Charlemagne, who came quickly into Italy, invested Pavia, the stronghold of Desiderius, and in six months destroyed the Lombard kingdom. Charlemagne then went to Rome, and not only restored to the Pope all his territories, but added to them several important provinces and the island of Corsica. So the Temporal Power of the Popes was established; and, if the whole matter be well looked into by the light of history, it will be seen, that the claims of the Popes to their possessions rested originally on a legitimate basis.

The Protestant Sismondi, as cited by Gosselin, says: "The more the Romans found themselves abandoned by the emperors, the more they attached themselves to the popes, who during this period were almost all Romans by birth, and who, from their eminent virtues, have been placed in the calendar of saints. The defence of Rome was regarded as a religious war, because the Lombards were either Arians or still attached to paganism; the popes, to protect their churches and convents from the profanation of those barbarians, employed all the ecclesiastical wealth at their disposal, and the alms which they obtained from the charity of the faithful of the West; so that the increasing power of those popes over the city of Rome was founded on the most legitimate of all titles, their virtues and their beneficence." (Ital. Rep., Vol. I. p. 122.)

"The reign of the popes, which gratified the prejudices, was not incompatible with the liberties, of Rome; and a more critical inquiry would have revealed a still nobler source of their power; the gratitude of a nation, whom they had rescued from the heresy and oppression of the Greek tyrant." (Gibbon's Hist., Vol. VI. p. 423.)

The history of the Papacy, during the Middle Ages, is a history of the highest moral intelligence, patiently but persistently engaged in bringing under rule and order the hordes of northern barbarians that inundated southern Europe; in curbing or controlling their wild passions, in interposing a bar between the tyrant and his victim, in interdicting with an authoritative voice the strife of sovereigns and their feudatory chiefs, in ameliorating the condition of the poor and oppressed, and in contending against half barbaric princes for its own position to do its own work. Nor were the organizing and the directing of the Crusades the least of its meritorious enterprises. To the Papacy belongs the credit and glory of saving Europe from the grasp of the Moslems, of maintaining the Cross against the Crescent. It was the only power in Europe that had the intelligence to conceive, as well as the address to conduct to a successful issue, so sagacious an emprise; and, as it was superior to tribal jealousies, it could erect a standard, to collect all the nations for a common undertaking. And Europe united was necessary to keep at bay the swarms of Moslems that again and again essayed to deluge Christendom.

The man, though, whose knowledge of history amounts to little more than the dim recollection of a few disconnected events that he long ago gleaned from his school primer, but never well understood, may find it very hard to set his conscience at rest about the conduct of that tyrant at Canossa, and perhaps some other similar incident equally outrageous! But what obliquity of judgment there must be in the man, who, after studying the disputes of the Henrys, the Fredericks, and the Philips, with the Popes, will not say that right and justice were invariably on the side of St. Peter's successors. What would have been the condition of Europe, if those tyrannical and libertine monarchs had not been checked in their courses?

Milman says: "It is impossible to conceive what had been the confusion, the lawlessness, the chaotic state of the middle ages, without the mediæval Papacy; and of the mediæval Papacy the real father is Gregory the Great." (L. C., Vol. II. p. 44.)

Hardwick expresses himself more guardedly. "It may have served, indeed, as a centralizing agent, to facilitate the fusion of discordant races; it may have proved itself in times of anarchy and ignorance a powerful instrument, and in some sort may have balanced the encroachments of the civil power." (M. A., p. 2.)

The Lutheran Hase says: "Accordingly in the tenth century when both the *hierarchy* and the *feudal monarchy* became strong, and when men no longer relied upon mere physical force, but contended with a youthful and romantic enthusiasm for honor, love, and faith, the church naturally became the supreme power of the age, because it was the educator of the people, and held in its hands all the treasures of spiritual grace for earth and heaven. Whenever it entered the lists against mere brute force it was of course defeated, but it always held the first place in the hearts of the people. . . . Every pope who understood his position must have felt that he was the protector of political freedom and the deliverer of all who were oppressed. The Germanic people became divided into different nations, and indeed every estate, every city, and every corporation endeavored to become independent. But the common connection of all nations and orders with the papacy united them together as one great Christian family, in whose general enterprises all distinctions were forgotten and national peculiarities were disregarded." (Ch. Hist., p. 182.)

Alzog quotes the Protestant Herder for this: "Were all the emperors, kings, princes, and cavaliers of Christendom obliged to make good the claims by which they rose to power, then might the man (the Pope) wearing the triple crown and adored at Rome, borne aloft upon the shoulders of peaceable priests, bless them, and say: 'Without me, you would not be what you are.' The Popes have preserved antiquity, and Rome should remain the peaceful sanctuary of the precious treasures of the past." ('Ideas,'

Vol. IV. p. 108.)

"We must not pass sentence on an institution without examining the opinion on which it is founded; and before we judge of the opinion, we must estimate the circumstances by which it was engendered. The disorganized state of Europe produced a strong opinion that some power for appeal and protection should be constituted; a power with intelligence to guide its decisions, and sanctity to enforce respect for them: the revived papacy seemed an institution suited to these conditions, and under the circumstances it was capable of being rendered the great instrument for reforming civil society." (Taylor's "Modern History," p. 402.) On the same page, Taylor says, concerning the measures of Pope Gregory VII., or Hildebrand, that "in the eleventh century, every one of these measures was necessary to counteract some evil principle, and milder or more justifiable means would not have been adequate to the occasion."

The following is by the Catholic De Maistre, as reported by Gosselin. "The authority of the popes was the power chosen and established during the middle ages as a counterpoise for the temporal power, to make it supportable to men. In this, there was certainly nothing contrary to the nature of things, which admits of every form of political association. If this power is not established, I do not mean to say that it ought to be established or reestablished; I have repeatedly made this solemn disclaimer: I merely assert, with reference to ancient times, that being established, it was as legitimate as any other; the sole foundation of all power being possession. The authority of popes over kings was disputed by none except those whom it judged. There never, therefore, was a more legitimate authority; because there never was one less disputed. What is there certain among men, if usage, especially when undisputed, is not the mother of legitimacy? It is the greatest of all sophisms to transport a modern system to ancient times, and to judge by that rule the men and affairs of ages more or less remote. Such a principle would upset the world: all possible established institutions could be subverted by that means, by judging them according to abstract theories; once admit that kings and peoples agreed in recognizing the authority of the popes, and all modern objections are refuted. During the course of my life, I have often heard the question asked, by what right the popes deposed emperors? the answer is easy: by the same right on which all legitimate authority reposes: *possession* on one side, and *assent* on the other."

The contents of these quotations, taken from authors of the highest intellectual authority, ought to convince the man with an equitable mind, that after all there may not be so much for exultant condemnation in the Temporal Power of the Popes, as some people may fancy.

LETTER VII.

"REFORMERS" AND THE "REFORMATION."

In this letter I intend to say a little about the "Reformers" and the "Reformation." Every body knows, that Luther, Zwingle, Calvin, Knox, and Cranmer were the heroes of the much belauded reform; and that, for the placid piety of their lives, for their judicious labors, for their intrepid zeal in denouncing error, and for their enlightened teachings, their successive disciples have lavished on their names the most extravagant encomiums. No one knows better than I, how offensive, how abhorrent, it is to the orthodox Protestant to hear any thing repeated, much less to see any thing entertained, that reflects upon the motives or the doings of these men; but, although I should be sorry to offend any one, I will here expose to view a little of what I found out about them, after I strayed from the histories of Foxe and of some others of the same animus.

The honor of originating the reform was disputed by the adherents of Luther and by those of Zwingle, for their respective masters; the Lutherans contending, that the latter was at best but a sorry expounder of Lutheranism, while the Switzers as stoutly maintained, that the only good Luther ever taught he learned from Zwingle. But posterity has unanimously, and no doubt fairly, conceded to the German the credit for which he so ardently craved and so boldly struggled. Luther's first movements appeared little like those of a man with a settled purpose or a firm conscience. Sometimes he was all for reform, then he would declare himself a submissive member of the Church; sometimes he was throwing down the gauntlet against the world, and as often he shrank into the most abject servility; he often gave away to fits of violent passion, and just as often he vowed to amend his conduct: but, by the nicest arts of dissimulation and the meanest hypocrisy, he gathered partisans to his side and warped circumstances to his own advantage. He caught the ear of the common people, by magnifying their grievances and exciting them to sedition: on their defeat he deserted them and then stormed for their destruction. But his new doctrines were very acceptable to the nobles, when they discovered that sacrilege and robbery were elevated into virtues. Seeing the success of his tactics, the powerful effect of his coarse harangues, and the numbers of his followers, he gave full scope to the suggestions of his ambition. The idea of forming a separate church, that had gradually taken shape in his mind, now so thoroughly engrossed and enchanted him, that he repelled with pious scorn every overture of peace and reconciliation. Fancy or invent whatever you like in his favor, it is undeniable and is admitted by many Protestants, that Luther was moved by ambition to form an independent church, and was extremely jealous lest any one else might share the glory with him. His chief reason for rejecting the dogmas of the Church was, that they are nothing but human opinions; and his recommending his own opinions instead gives us a fair idea of his unruffled cheek. But his new bundle of doctrines involved him in a perplexity of labors. At best but a farrago of crude conceits, it required for its support, first a re-judgment of the canon of Scripture, then a list of the books graduated according to the authority of each, and finally a special translation. Lutheranism needed a Lutheran Bible! But it is strange, that, if Luther was, as he had the hardihood to assert, divinely commissioned to announce the whole scriptural truth, he could be prevailed on in any way to change or even modify what he had distinctly asserted. The Catholics are sometimes sneered at for using "the stock argument," that truth is unchangeable. Catholics are not the only ones that use it. Guizot says, "It is moreover permanent, and always the same, *for truth is unchangeable.*" Nor will any one quarrel with him for saying so. It is an axiom that no sober man will dispute. But Luther changed and changed; and his followers have changed and re-changed. I do not purpose to say much about the particular tenets of Lutheranism: I merely observe, that, either owing to the arguments of Catholics, or to the whimsical moods of the Lutherans, they have been repeatedly changed. And this ought to convince any man, that the Holy Ghost, the Spirit of Truth, has had little to do with Lutheranism. But then Luther was such a pure-minded son of righteousness and so exemplary in his habits and sobriety of life, that his teachings might be accepted out of respect to the person. Some such idea must surely be entertained by the people that admit his contradictions, but yet invoke his name. Was Luther, however, a pattern of morality and a reflection of all the virtues?

Alzog quotes the Protestant Ancillon for this: "His (Luther's) acts were the result of passion, rather than the outgrowth of fixed principles; and if, on the one hand, his character was not soiled by degrading vice, on the other, it was not ennobled by distinguished virtue. On the whole, admitting that he was gifted with genius, it cannot be denied that he was destitute of moral qualities of a high order." According to the same historian, Count Hoyer of Mansfield said this: "I have been all along, as I was at Worms, a good Lutheran; but I have learned that Luther is a blackguard, and as good a drunkard as there is in Mansfield, delighting to be in the company of beautiful women and to play upon his flute. His conduct is unbecoming, and he seems irretrievably fallen." That he could not get along without "Katie" is no great proof that his affections were purely spiritual, nor is it a testimonial to his saintliness that he violated a solemn vow of celibacy, to embrace her. His native tendencies are plainly exposed in his famous sermon on matrimony; some specimen sentences of which I would quote but for the fact, that they are too filthy to repeat. When I first read Bossuet's "Variations," I noticed what he says about Luther's giving Philip of Hesse permission to take a second wife, while his first was still living; but at that time I looked upon it as an opposition calumny. It is true enough however; and the Lutherans were distinctly reminded of it, by Cranmer, when they took a virtuous stand against the divorce desired by Henry VIII. "But that Melancthon, and other German divines, were not very orthodox in this, and some other matters, appears from Cranmer's letter to Osiander. In this letter, 'he complains of the loose casuistry and mistaken opinions of the German divines, and what scandal they gave to the reformation. For this purpose, he tells us, they allowed the younger sons of noblemen to entertain strumpets, to prevent the parcelling out their estates, and lessening the figure of the elder family: that divines who allow this liberty, were altogether unqualified to make invectives against any indulgence in the Church of Rome. Further, I desire,' says he, 'to know what excuse can be made for your permission of a second marriage after divorce, while both the parties were living; and, which is still worse, you allow a man a plurality of wives without the ceremony of a divorce. That this is matter of fact, you acquainted me, as I remember, in some of your letters, adding withal, that Melancthon himself was present at one of these second weddings, and gave countenance to it.'" (Collier's Hist., Vol. IV. p. 156.) "On the other hand, we have the single fact of the bigamy of the Landgrave, for the secret consummation of which Luther and his colleagues granted a dispensation." (Hase's Ch. Hist., p. 440.) (See also Imperial Biog. Dict., Art. *Philip of Hesse*; or Cate's Biog. Dict.) Of it Luther said: "*Ego sane fateor me non posse prohibere si quis velit plures ducere uxores, nec repugnat sacris literis.*" Sir William Hamilton says, that Luther held "polygamy as a religious speculation." And yet it is likely, that, after Melancthon, Luther was morally the best of the "Reformers." Concerning his literary work, Hallam says: "But from the Latin works of Luther few readers, I believe, will rise without disappointment. Their intemperance, their coarseness, their inelegance, their scurillity, their wild paradoxes, that menace the foundations of religious morality, are not compensated, so far at least as my slight acquaintance with them extends, by much strength or acuteness, and still less by any impressive eloquence. Some of his treatises, and we may instance his reply to Henry VIII., or the book against 'the falsely named order of bishops,' can be described as little else than bellowing in bad Latin. Neither of these books display, so far as I can judge, any striking ability." (Hist. of Lit., Vol I. p. 192.) Elsewhere Hallam has: "The Lutherans, a narrow minded, intolerant faction." Luther prophesied too; but one of his vaticinal ventures has not so far been wholly fulfilled. In one of his transports, he said, referring to the Pope: "*Pestis eram vivus, moriens ero mors tua, papa!*" But he made a luckier hit, when he declared of his followers: "*Adorabunt stercora nostra et pro balsamo habebunt.*"

The "Pope of Geneva" has had a train of sturdy admirers, who would place his Institutes side by side with any thing that St. Paul ever wrote; and who think, that his sour, cold-blooded piety invested his manual with a halo of sanctity that enhances it above all earthly value. As I am not concerning myself with particular matters of faith, I will not give any of his revolting tenets. It is sufficient to notice, that, according to Calvin, neither Luther nor Zwingle had understood what the reform ought to be, nor what are the revealed truths of Christianity. The apostolic truths had to be discovered and thrown into a scientific form, by Calvin. Behold the work finally accomplished, then, in the Institutes. Yet there are diversities of opinions ('human') as to the worth of the Institutes. Collier, in the preface to the fourth volume of his History, makes this impious assertion: "In my humble opinion, Coke's Institutes would be better furniture (for the Anglican clergy) than Calvin's Institutions; and the reading of the Statute-book much more serviceable than some systems of Dutch divinity." Hase, in his Hist., p. 408, says, that the Lutherans "looked upon Calvinism as only a bridge to Mohammedanism." But to Calvin, who also took a wife, a widow (most of the Helvetic lights took to widows), we are indebted for one expression that well explains, in most cases, the cause of clerical apostasy; and no reformer but Calvin would have gratified his vindictiveness, by putting the opinion in words. For some reason, he cherished, as only Calvin could cherish, a bitter hatred of one Bernard, a Franciscan; and, when this Bernard came into the reform and confirmed his sincerity, by breaking his vows in taking a wife, Calvin, instead of proffering the hand of reconciliation, indulged his malice by saying: "He (Bernard) was always hostile to it (reform) till he beheld Christ in a handsome wife." (Dyer's Life of C., p. 104.) By reading the history of his rule in Geneva, any one can easily discover the true character of Calvin. His treatment of Castellio, Bolsec, Ameaux, Gruet, Gentilis, Berthelier, and his rampant savagery in burning Servetus, plainly show that he was destitute of pity, mercy, and humanity.

His disciple, John Knox, whom Dr. Johnson called "The Ruffian of the Reformation," is entitled to civil consideration only in comparison with his master. Spalding repeats Whittaker, a Protestant, who speaks of Knox, as "a fanatical incendiary, a holy savage, the sow of violence and barbarism, the religious Sachem of religious Mohawks." Perhaps Collier flatters him a little: "To deal plainly with his memory, he was a flaming incendiary, maintained desperate principles, and made no scruple to put them in practice. He had no small share in fomenting the rebellion against the queen, in embroiling the kingdom, and making it a scene of blood and confusion for near seven years together." (Vol. VI. p. 515.) He says (Vol. IX. p. 448.) in addition: "In fine, false principles, short learning, flaming heat, and extravagant assurance, are part of Knox's character; and I am sorry matter of fact will make it no better. . . . . To sum up this matter in a word or two; upon Luther I shall observe nothing further, but as to Calvin and the rest, their reputation has not been serviceable in some respects: neither have their writings had any kind effect upon the repose of Christendom." "In a conversation with Maitland, he (Knox) asserted most explicitly the duty of putting idolaters to death. Nothing can be more sanguinary than the

Reformer's spirit in this remarkable interview. . . . It is strange to see men, professing all the while our modern creed of charity and toleration, extol these blood-thirsty bull-dogs of the 16th century." (Hallam's Const. Hist., Vol. I. p. 190.) Knox also matrimonied—twice. In the "Imperial Biographical Dictionary," there is a fairly full Life of Knox, written by the Presbyterian, Rev. John Eadie, D.D., of Glasgow, who gives a very interesting morsel about John's second venture. "In March, 1564, Knox, who had been three years a widower, and was now on the verge of *sixty*, married Margaret Stewart, daughter of Lord Ochiltree—his lordship being a descendant of Robert, duke of Albany, second son of King Robert II. Popish writers aver that he gained the young lady's heart by witchcraft, for she was little more than *twenty*. Nicol Burne describes him as going to Lord Ochiltree's mansion 'not lyke an auld decrepit priest, as he was, but lyke as he had been ane of the bluid-royal, with his bendis of taffetie feschnit with golden rings and precious stanes.'"

The English "Reformer," Cranmer, was the outraged innocent that said, "This hand hath offended." He was the great Protestant martyr! Luther, Melancthon, Zwingle, Calvin, even Knox, and other worthies of the "Reform," braved with impunity "the remorseless fury of the Catholics;" but the sainted Cranmer sealed his faith with his death! Foxe, whom no one believes, has given us a flaming picture of England's great "Reformer" burning at the stake. Sure enough, it was a cruel death; but, if any man ever deserved to be burnt, that man was Cranmer. The Lutherans, who called those who suffered in Mary's reign "The Devil's Martyrs," gave him a place. The particulars of his life show that he was practically a common pimp, a perjured ecclesiastic, a dissimulator of his faith, a bloody persecutor, a pliant tool for any one that could command him, and a treasonable subject. Macaulay, in his review of Hallam's Const. Hist., says all that is necessary to know Cranmer. I can give only a few extracts. "Cranmer rose into favor by serving Henry in the disgraceful affair of his first divorce. He promoted the marriage of Anne Boleyn with the king. On a frivolous pretence he pronounced that marriage null and void. On a pretence, if possible, still more frivolous, he dissolved the ties which bound the shameless tyrant to Anne of Cleves. He attached himself to Cromwell while the fortunes of Cromwell flourished. He voted for cutting off Cromwell's head without a trial, when the tide of royal favor turned. He conformed backwards and forwards as the King changed his mind. He assisted, while Henry lived, in condemning to the flames those who denied the doctrine of transubstantiation. He found out, as soon as Henry was dead, that the doctrine was false. He was, however, not at a loss for people to burn. The authority of his station and of his gray hairs was employed to overcome the disgust with which an intelligent and virtuous child regarded persecution. . . Equally false to political and to religious obligations, the primate was first the tool of Somerset, and then the tool of Northumberland. When the Protector wished to put his own brother to death, without even the semblance of a trial, he found a ready instrument in Cranmer. In spite of the canon law, which forbade a churchman to take any part in matters of blood, the archbishop signed the warrant for the atrocious sentence. When Somerset had been in his turn destroyed, his destroyer received the support of Cranmer in a wicked attempt to change the course of the succession. . . If Cranmer had shown half as much firmness when Edward requested him to commit treason as he had before shown when Edward requested him not to commit murder, he might have saved the country from one of the greatest misfortunes (Marian persecution) that it ever underwent. He became, from whatever motive, the accomplice of the worthless Dudley. The virtuous scruples of another young and amiable mind were to be overcome. As Edward had been forced into persecution, Jane was to be seduced into treason. . . To the part which Cranmer, and unfortunately some better men than Cranmer, took in this most reprehensible scheme, much of the severity with which the Protestants were afterwards treated must in fairness be ascribed. . . But his martyrdom, it is said, redeemed every thing. It is extraordinary that so much ignorance should exist on this subject. The fact is that, if a martyr be a man who chooses to die rather than to renounce his opinions, Cranmer was no more a martyr than Dr. Dodd. He died solely because he could not help it. He never retracted his recantation, till he found he had made it in vain. The Queen was fully resolved that, Catholic or Protestant, he should burn. Then he spoke out, as people generally speak out when they are at the point of death and have nothing to hope or to fear on earth. If Mary had suffered him to live, we suspect that he would have heard mass and received absolution, like a good Catholic, till the accession of Elizabeth, and that he would then have purchased, by another apostasy, the power of burning men better and braver than himself." Hallam says that Cranmer recanted no less than six times. Yet between his recantations he found time to concoct out of his own head a catechism, to collect from Catholic books the matter for a new liturgy, and to draw up articles of faith. And, although he declared, when he was engaged in these labors, that he was "under the inspiration of the Holy Ghost," like all the other "Reformers" he was continually making radical changes in his work. But it may be in his favor, that he was only a subordinate. Henry, while he lived, was the ruling mind of "the glorious Reformation," and after his death others nearly as imperious overawed poor Cranmer. Macaulay says: "The work (reform) which had been begun by Henry, the murderer of his wives, was continued by Somerset, the murderer of his brother, and completed by Elizabeth, the murderer of her guest."

Queen Bess, the "Occidental Star," is the Protestant Virgin. Greene, Hist., p. 376, speaks of her: "Her levity, her frivolous laughter, her unwomanly jests gave color to a thousand scandals. Her character, in fact, like her portraits, was utterly without shade. Of womanly reserve or self-restraint she knew nothing. No instinct of delicacy veiled the voluptuous temper which had broken out in the romps of her girlhood, and showed itself almost ostentatiously throughout her later life. Personal beauty in a man was a sure passport to her liking. She patted handsome young squires on the neck when they knelt to kiss her hand, and fondled her "sweet Robin," Lord Leicester, in the face of the Court." Again: "Nothing is more revolting in the Queen, but nothing is more characteristic, than her shameless mendacity. It was an age of political lying, but in the profusion and recklessness of her lies Elizabeth stood without a peer in Christendom. A falsehood was to her simply an intellectual means of meeting a difficulty; and the ease with which she asserted or denied whatever suited her purpose was only equaled by the cynical indifference with which she met the exposure of her lies as soon as their purpose was answered." (p. 378.) Her suspicious virtue she probably inherited from her mother, her innate cruelty from her father, but her duplicity and constant lying seem to have been acquired habits.

Now, then, look at the sanctified scoundrels that pretended to effect a reformation in religion; the canting gospellers that revelled in plunder, gloried in sacrilege and lechery, and practised every form of hypocrisy, cruelty, and vice, that is loathsome and revolting. The sins of any one of them were sufficient to sink to perdition the whole reform tribe, and how any one but half conversant with their characters and doings can honor their names or respect their memories is more than I can understand.

The reform appeared in five parties, and each party, in the fullness of its enlightened piety and charity, condemned and hated the other four. And this, mind, was in the very beginning of the reform. Trace any one of these parties down to the present, and what is its history?—bitter upbraidings from members of its own bosom, because it had never learned the gospel truths; and the quarrel invariably terminated in a split. The first party had a split; each of the splits has had its own split; and so on. The result is, that not one of the original parties can be found to-day, teaching its first distinctive doctrines. What were at first "the fundamental truths" are now silently ignored or stoutly contradicted. Lutheranism is dead: the Anabaptists—where are they? Both Supralapsarianism and Infralapsarianism are too austere for profitable use in this enlightened age; and Anglicanism has so far strayed from the path chalked out by Cranmer and his coadjutors, that, according to the latest reports, it has actually battled its way into "Catholicism."

Protestantism in history is a picture of contemptible wranglings, of implacable feuds, of beastly scandals, of stalwart lying, of rough jostlings for first place to snatch plunder, and of heartless indifference to the cares and the necessities of the indigent and the helpless. But the climax of utter nonsense is reached, when the words, Protestantism and Truth, are coupled together. What men have ever handled the Truth as the Protestants have handled Religion? And what is Protestantism to-day? If the man in the moon were to drop down amongst the Protestants, to learn the religion of Christ, what would be his experience? Every one of the hundred and more sects would tell him a story different from that of any other sect, and append to it the salutary caution that he must be on his guard against the representations of every other denomination. I think that before the old man would be half through with his inquiries, he would be made, by the varied contradictions, what thousands upon thousands of to-day have been made, a doubter; he would regret that he ever ventured on such a useless trip, and would heartily wish himself back home again. I once heard a preacher say that this multiplicity of denominations and creeds is conducive to—I forget what; but his explanation, I thought, would have been briefer, more open to comprehension, and more in agreement with facts, had he simply repeated the commercial maxim, that competition is the life of trade. But St. Paul condemned Protestantism long ago. He said: "Now I beseech you, brethren, by the name of our Lord Jesus Christ, that ye all speak the same thing, and that there be no divisions among you; but that ye be perfectly joined together in the same mind and in the same judgment." Palmer, in his "Treatise on the Church," has: "The divisions of modern sects calling themselves Protestant, afford a strong argument for the necessity of submission to the judgment of the universal church; for, surely, it is impossible that Christ could have designed his disciples to break into a hundred different sects, contending with each other on every doctrine of religion. It is impossible, I say, that this system of endless division can be christian. It cannot but be the result of some deep-rooted, some universal error, some radically false principle which is common to all these sects. And what principle *do* they hold in common, except the right of each individual to oppose his judgment to that of all the church? This principle, then, must be utterly false and unfounded." (Vol. II. p. 113.)

And the working and the results of the "Reformation" have not always been viewed with unmixed satisfaction by many of its greatest advocates. Collier (Vol., VIII. p. 338.), says: "And thus the Presbyterians having embroiled the kingdoms, kindled and carried on a calamitous war, during which, more seats were plundered and burnt, more churches robbed and profaned, more blood spilt, within the compass of four years; and, in short, more frightful scenes opened of ravage, of slaughter and confusion, than had been acted in the long contest between the houses of York and Lancaster; the Presbyterians, I say, after having thrown their country into all this misery and convulsion, met with nothing but infamy and disappointment. For after having wrested the sword out of the king's hands, and brought the rebellion to their wishes, when they thought of nothing less than dividing the prey, and raising vast fortunes out of crown and church lands, their hopes were suddenly scattered, they were turned out of their scandalous acquisitions, and publicly exposed to contempt and scorn. For now the Independents forced them to retire from Westminster, seized their posts, and made themselves masters, upon the matter, both in Church and State. But of this more afterwards. As for religion, it was in no better condition than civil interest: the Presbyterians preached up the purity and the power, till they left neither. I shall make a report of this matter from an eminent champion for the cause: it is Edwards, who wrote the 'Gangræna;' a book in which the errors, heresies, blasphemies, and lewd practice, which broke out in the last four years, are recited. . . . A man thus well affected, we may be sure would not make things worse than they were, nor paint the new reformation in the hardest complexion. Let us hear then what account the gentleman gives of this matter." Collier then gives Edward's lamentation as follows: "Things every day grow worse and worse; you can hardly imagine them so bad as they are. No kind of blasphemy, heresy, disorder, and confusion, but it is found among us, or coming in upon us. For we, instead of reformation, are grown from one extreme to another; fallen from Scylla to Charybdis; from popish innovations, superstitions, and prelatical tyranny, to damnable heresies, horrid blasphemies, libertinism, and fearful anarchy. Our evils are not removed and cured, but only changed: one disease and devil hath left us, and another as bad is come in the room. Yea, this last extremity into which we are fallen, is far more high, violent, and dangerous, in many respects, &c. Have we not a deformation, and worse things come in upon us than ever we had before? Were any of those monsters heard of heretofore, which are now common amongst us, as denying the Scriptures, &c.? You have broken down the images of the Trinity, Virgin Mary, Apostles; and we have those who overthrow the doctrine of the Trinity, oppose the divinity of Christ, speak evil of the Virgin Mary, and slight the Apostles. You have cast out the bishops and their officers, and we have many that cast down to the ground all ministers in all the reformed Churches. You have cast out ceremonies in the sacraments, as the cross, kneeling at the Lord's Supper; and we have many who cast out the sacraments of baptism and the Lord's Supper. You have put down saints' days, and we have many who make nothing at all of the Lord's-day, and fast-days. You have taken away the superfluous, excessive maintenance of bishops and deans, and we have many that take away and cry down the necessary maintenance of ministers. In the bishops' days we had singing of psalms taken away in some places, conceived prayer and preaching, and, in their room, anthems, stinted forms, and reading brought in: and now we have singing of psalms spoken against, and cast out of some churches: yea, all public prayer questioned, and all ministerial preaching denied. In the bishops' time, popish innovations were introduced, as bowing at altars, &c.: and now we have anointing the sick with oil. Then we had bishoping of children, now we have bishoping of men and women, by strange laying on of hands. In the bishops' days we had many unlearned ministers; and have we not now a company of Jeroboam's priests? In the bishops' days we had the fourth commandment taken away; but now we have all the ten commandments at once, by the Antinomians; yea, all faith and the Gospel denied. The worst of the prelates, in the midst of many popish, Arminian tenets, and popish innovations, held many sound doctrines, and had many commendable practices: yea, the very Papists hold and keep to many articles of faith and truths of God, have some order amongst them, encourage learning, have certain fixed principles of truth, with practices of devotion and good works; but many of the sects and sectaries in our days deny all principle of religion, are enemies to all holy duties, order, learning, overthrowing all; being 'vertiginosi spiritus,' whirligig spirits. And the great opinion of an universal toleration tends to the laying all waste, and dissolution of all religion and good manners, &c. What swarms are there of all sorts of illiterate mechanic preachers; yea, of women and boy preachers: what liberty of preaching, printing of all errors, or for a toleration of all, and against the Directory, Covenant, monthly fast, Presbyterial government, and all ordinances of parliament in reference to religion?—These sectaries have been growing upon us, ever since the first year of our sitting, and have every year increased more and more."

If, in this sweeping condemnation of the sects, he included the sainted Puritan, he must have been more zealous than just; since the Puritans must have been of all men the most severely conscientious. In the "Book of Discipline" was this: "Let persuasions be used, that such names that do savour either of paganism or popery be not given to children at their baptism, but principally those whereof there are examples in the Scriptures." Collier (Vol. VII. p. 138.) says: "The Puritans were very strict in keeping close to this rule, as may be collected from the odd names they gave their children: such as 'The Lord is near,' 'More Trial,' 'Reformation,' 'Discipline,' 'Joy again,' 'Sufficient,' 'From above,' 'Free Gifts,' 'More Fruit,' 'Dust,' &c. And here Snape was remarkably scrupulous: for this minister refused to baptize one Christopher Hodkinson's child, because he would have it christened Richard. Snape acquainted Hodkinson with his opinion beforehand: he told him he must change the name, and look out for one in the Scripture. But the father, not thinking this fancy would be so strongly insisted on, brought his son to church. Snape proceeded in the solemnity till he came to naming the child, but, not being able to prevail for any other name than Richard, refused to administer the sacrament; and thus the child was carried away, and afterwards baptized by a conforming clergyman."

But the man whose horizon is limited to the boundaries of his own township, and whose knowledge of the past runs no farther back than the revel at his grandfather's silver wedding, may carry about with him the magnificent idea, that, whether true or false, Protestantism in its career has been steadily increasing, and is rapidly becoming the dominant institution of the universe. His idea would be countenanced only by some miserable sectarian weekly. It is granted all around, that Protestantism, since its first violent out-burst, has made no conquests. Greene, Hist., p. 468, says: "But at the very instant of its seeming triumph, the advance of the new religion was suddenly arrested. The first twenty years of Elizabeth's reign were a period of suspense. The progress of Protestantism gradually ceased. It wasted its strength in theological controversies and persecutions, above all in the bitter and venomous discussions between the Churches which followed Luther and the Churches which followed Calvin. It was degraded and weakened by the prostitution of the Reformation to political ends, by the greed and worthlessness of the German princes who espoused its cause, by the factious lawlessness of the nobles in Poland and of the Huguenots in France." On page 469, there is: "Even learning passed gradually over to the side of the older faith. Bellarmine, the greatest of controversialists at this time, Baronius, the most erudite of Church historians, were both Catholics." For confirmation of the same fact, Macaulay's critique of Ranke's 'Popes' may be examined.

What good has Protestantism achieved? Within two hundred years it has not converted a single tribe; it has never made a move towards helping those who have not been able to help themselves; it has erected no institutions; it has never dreamed of any thing like the Truce of God; and, instead of impressing a people with the obligations of charity and forbearance towards one another, it has more generally succeeded in sowing the seeds of dissension and strife. It has been a success only, first as a devastator, and afterwards as an obstacle. The general cry, that to Protestantism we owe all our liberty, is arrant nonsense. Guizot, Hist. of Civ., says: "In Germany there was no political liberty; the Reformation did not introduce it; it rather strengthened than enfeebled the power of princes; it was rather opposed to the free institutions of the middle ages than favorable to their progress." (p. 227.) The "Reformers" allied themselves with princes to crush the common people; and as for religious liberty every page of the reform history shows, that the "Reformers" brought into use every power and plan to force into the people the new doctrines. A quotation from Hallam will be in order here: "Whatever may be the bias of our minds as to the truth of Luther's doctrines, we should be careful, in considering the Reformation as a part of the history of mankind, not to be misled by the superficial and ungrounded representations which we sometimes find in modern writers. Such is this, that Luther, struck by the absurdity of the prevailing superstitions, was desirous of introducing a more rational system of religion; or, that he contended for freedom of inquiry, and the boundless privileges of individual judgment; or, what others have been pleased to suggest, that his zeal for learning and ancient philosophy led him to attack the ignorance of the monks and the crafty policy of the church, which withstood all liberal studies. These notions are merely fallacious refinements, as every man of plain understanding, who is acquainted with the writings of the early reformers, or has considered their history, must acknowledge." (Hist. of Lit., Vol. I. p. 165.) Balmez shows plainly that Protestantism is the offspring, and not the cause, of private judgment. In his own masterly way he says truly: "The essential principle of Protestantism is one of destruction; this is the cause of its incessant variations, of its dissolution and annihilation. As a particular religion it no longer exists, for it has no peculiar faith, no positive character, no government, nothing that is essential to form an existence; Protestantism is only a negative. If there is anything to be found in it of a positive nature, it is nothing more than vestiges and ruins; all is without force, without action, without the spirit of life. It cannot show an edifice raised by its own hands, it cannot, like Catholicity, stand in the midst of its vast works and say, 'These are mine.' Protestantism can only sit down on a heap of ruins, and say with truth, 'I have made this pile.'" ("Protestantism and Catholicity Compared," p. 69.)

LETTER VIII.

REVIEW AND ADVANCE.

So far, I have in a cursory manner looked at Catholicity and Protestantism as they appear in history; and have, as nearly as I have been able, strictly adhered, up to this, to my first rambling course of study. From this point I took a retrospect of both. But, when I could, with a clear eye, look back upon them and see them as they have been—Catholicity as it has moved, with a steadfast aim and undiverted steps, from the very beginning of Christianity down through all the ages to the present; often opposed, often assailed, but with the shouts of victory always on its lips; alluring to its side the wisest, and, after making them the best and noblest, sending them back into the world, to spend the remainder of their lives in doing deeds of mercy and benevolence; ever extending its empire and influence among the nations, and infusing into them a spirit of culture and progress, that raised them from barbarism to the highest state of civilization; bearing on its fostering bosom the weak and the decrepit, and giving to friend and foe alike, in the hour of distress, a generous welcome and the tenderest care; and holding aloft for the benefit and encouragement of all the torch of learning and the ensigns of true liberty: and Protestantism, a name that designates nothing that will outlast a day; that has been a cloak for every theological phantasy and a shelter for every imaginable form of fanaticism; that has lamentably failed to exhibit in its principles and professions consistency or sincerity, and has signally miscarried in all its serious undertakings; and whose short but turbulent history shows to a demonstration, that, whatever else it may have been, it has been, what it is to-day, a confusion of tongues and a kingdom divided against itself—when, I say, I looked back upon both and saw all this, the blind reverence for Protestantism, to which I had been so carefully trained, left me altogether; and for Catholicity, a word which for the greater part of my life I had delighted to ridicule, I had something above common respect. And this made a Catholic of me? Nothing of the sort, my friend. I was too heavily handicapped with inveterate prejudices to surrender so readily. I could not very well have read many ecclesiastical books without coming across, and paying some slight attention to, occasional discussions of doctrine; but further than the general opinion, that the Catholics, being always and every where the same in faith, have all the probabilities in their favor, against the Protestants with their ever-changing opinions, I had not advanced. I had adopted no tenet nor dogma peculiarly Catholic; but in the matter of belief I had made one certain discovery, that there is, what there should be, one body of Christians who have *never* been "tossed about by every wind of doctrine." For the first time I halted. It was high time to do so; for I saw well enough, that I was on the broad road to "Popery." And, when I plainly realized the fact, I shrank within myself. This revulsion I can impute to nothing but an uprising of ingrained prejudices. On every side I looked for an excuse to make a halt. I had often heard it said, that the principles and the representations of the Catholics are wonderfully seductive to those that are not specially trained to meet them. But this, the best I could lay my hands on, could not apply to me, since I had examined hardly any thing so far but dry historical facts. A better one came at last; the rapid change in my knowledge of church affairs had produced too great a reaction; a little enthusiasm, or something like it, had, perhaps, overlaid my judgment. No doubt I had been going too fast and too inconsiderately. I would take a rest. But rest I could not. All day long and a good part of the night, I was roving into the past and looking into the condition of the present. Satisfied, though, as I was, that the Protestants are no safe guides in Christianity, I had not the courage to examine the teachings of the Church. I dreaded the possible result. What would be said, if I should turn "Papist?" Could I not admire the Catholic Church, in secret though, if I liked, and give Protestantism a civil go-by? For a time I was completely nonplussed.

One day while I was in this halting state, I was told by a person with whom I was having a talk on the subject of churches, that it makes no difference whatever to what church a man belongs, provided he lives a virtuous life. As I was not prepared to dispute it on the spot, I took it home, to look at it. At that time I was, from lack of information, altogether unqualified to consider the subject; but I did not fail to see, that it is a remarkable statement for a solifidian to make, and that, even if it can be maintained, it tells as much for the Catholic Church as for any other.

A Doctor of Medicine told me, that the difficulty about the churches has its root in the theologies! His idea was to abolish theology entirely and to take the Word of God in its purity and simplicity. Then there would be concord and peace. But, I asked myself, is it possible for a Christian to be without a theology? To be a Christian a man must have faith; he must believe something; and this something, always an aggregation of truths, when confessed in a full and systematic manner, makes a theology. A small one it may be, but a theology nevertheless. His idea was no good to me.

Shortly after this I chanced to read, in the "Westminster Review," a critique of Butler's "Analogy," written, I judged, by one that was neither a Catholic nor a Protestant. He seemed to be a clear-headed neutral. He told me this: "In the first chapter of the second part we have a long paragraph on the importance of a 'visible church.' Without such a visible Church, the 'repository of the Oracles of God,' the author tells us that Christianity must 'in a great degree have been sunk and forgot in a very few ages.' Some observations might be made upon this statement, if taken in conjunction with others contained in the book: however, the chief point to notice here is that Butler insists with great force upon the necessity and importance of a *visible Church*. This being so, where are we to look for this 'city upon a hill,' this 'standing memorial to the world of the duty which we owe to our Maker?' Of course, it might be argued, on the principles of the Analogy, that this Church *may* be the Church of England as by law established. That is to say, objections to its being the Church of England might be shown to be inconclusive, as similar objections to Christianity have been shown to be. Or the Society of Friends, or the Unitarian body, may each be shown to be *possibly* this Church, on like principles. Now we think the claim of the Roman Catholic Church to occupy this position is one which at least merits attention; and we should be curious to know what objections can be raised against this claim, while we are of opinion that many positive arguments of great strength might be adduced in its favour. What is the principal objection which Protestants make to the Catholic Church? That some of its doctrines are not mentioned in the New Testament. Granting this—though it can only be granted with the reservation that all its chief doctrines, for instance, the foundation of the Church on Peter, transubstantiation, purgatory, extreme unction, are either expressly contained in or else implied in the New Testament: at least mentioned in such a way that if they are not held to be implied, so neither can many of the chief dogmas retained by Protestantism be held to be sanctioned—yet, granting this, what does the omission amount to? We are nowhere informed that the New Testament contains the whole body of Christian doctrine. And it is clear that it does not: that it consists of a series of narratives and letters, the latter in particular referring to a body of doctrines entrusted to the keeping of a visible Church. What is required to be shown is that these Roman Catholic doctrines are *contrary* to Scripture; and this cannot be shown. Granting even that they were not fully developed at the time when most or all of the New Testament books had been written, this, on the supposition of a visible Church having been constituted, would offer no sort of difficulty. This gradual development of doctrine is strictly in accordance with what we gather from the Analogy of Nature. We are in no respect judges of the way in which it might have pleased God Almighty to communicate his revelation to mankind: at any rate, this is Butler's own argument. It might have been—judging from Analogy, we should infer that it would be likely to be—communicated in a gradual way. Thus, the dogma of the Immaculate Conception of the Virgin, in no respect opposed to the text of Scripture, might very well have been left to be brought to the light, after a long process of incubation, by this same visible Church. And with regard to other doctrines formulated at an earlier period, such for example as the invocation of Saints, it is absolutely ludicrous to contend that they are unscriptural, or that they substitute another kind of mediation for that of Christ: for if Paul prayed for his converts, if the prayer of faith saves the sick, if the prayer of a righteous man avails, it is idle, and indeed wholly without warrant from Scripture to affirm positively that prayers and supplications offered up by those who have put off this temporary garb of flesh can do nothing.

"Now, the Church of Rome presents herself to us not

only with many of the signs and appearances which we should expect to find in a visible Church, these signs and appearances being noted in her alone, but with the positive assurance that she and she alone is *the* visible Church. She informs us, as a consequence of this, that only for those within her pale is there a reasonable hope of salvation. If this claim can be absolutely disproved or shown to be ridiculous, there is an end to it, as under similar circumstances there would be an end to Christianity. But no reasonable man supposes that anything of the kind can be done in either case. Sane Protestants are therefore, on the grounds set forth in the Analogy, bound at least to comport themselves towards the Roman Catholic system in the same way as the author declares that sceptics are bound to comport themselves towards Christianity in general. 'A doubting apprehension that it may be true' will lay them under serious obligations to it: compel 'a reverend regard' to it under this doubtfulness, 'a regard not the same exactly, but in many respects nearly the same with what a full conviction of its truth would lay them under.' But we may go further than this. One of the strongest pleas urged by Bishop Butler with the view of inducing people to embrace Christianity is the prudential one. It is, on the whole, he says, the safer side to take. It is safer to act as though it were true, even although the judgment may be unconvinced. 'A mistake on one side may be in its consequences much more dangerous than one on the other. And what course is *most safe*, and what most dangerous is a consideration thought very material, when we deliberate not concerning events, but concerning conduct, in our temporal affair.' (Pt. II. ch. 7.) 'For supposing it doubtful, what would be the consequence of acting in this, or in a contrary manner: still that taking one side could be attended with little or no bad consequence, and taking the other might be attended with the greatest, must appear to unprejudiced reason of the highest moment towards determining how we are to act.' (*Ib.*) Now surely, if this be so, prudence requires us to embrace not only Christianity in general, but Roman Catholicism in particular. It is not held by Protestants that all Roman Catholics will be damned: at any rate the system of Protestantism does not require this: whereas the Roman Catholic system does certainly include the converse. It is therefore by far the safest course to conform to Rome. Nor do we see any way out of this except on the supposition that the claims of the latter can be confuted with a directness of proof which (as we have just said) is not forthcoming." (No. CCI.)

If I remember well, this had considerable effect in determining me to return to work. What am I, I thought, if the privilege of thinking and acting for myself be not mine? Whose business is it but my own? If I should finally be convinced that Catholicity is, what the Catholics say, the only true form of Christianity, am I a craven that I should be deterred from adopting it, by the sneers and taunts of those who put "religious liberty" on their banners? Besides, I had to go forward; or worse, back.

In beginning to study the Catholic belief, I pitched on, what I considered the hardest subject, transubstantiation. Fredet's "Eucharistic Mystery" was the little book that I first read on this dogma. How often we hear it said, that the Catholic faith is not scriptural! Fredet's book surprised me: in it I saw what I had never expected to see, that Scripture and Scripture alone soundly establishes the truth of the Catholic teaching on this subject. When I had finished with this book, I was thoroughly convinced that outside of the Catholic Church there can be no Holy Communion.

Were I to trace the "successive steps," as I intimated at first, I should here present some of the proofs that sustain this dogma; but they will be more in place hereafter.

While reading Frelet's book and other books, I was for a long time puzzled to understand how it is that Catholics attach so much importance to the authority of the Church. "It is the teaching of the Church" and "approved by the Church" were constantly occurring expressions that I did not understand. I had to learn the Catholic conception of the Church. In the next letter can be seen what I collected on the subject.

LETTER IX.

THE CHURCH.

"Art Thou a King then?" Pilate asked Jesus. The reply was: "For this cause came I into the world." The mission of Christ was to organize, to instruct, and to delegate divine power and authority to, a society of men who were to preach salvation to the whole human race, for all time to come. They were His disciples: He was their King. He likened His Kingdom to a field producing wheat and tares together, to a net that gathers of every kind, to a floor on which are wheat and chaff, to a marriage feast at which some have wedding garments and some have them not. The Scriptures show that this Kingdom is the Church. The word *ecclesia* (church), which signifies what is called forth, is used in the Testament, in different senses (Cat. Trent, p. 71.); but Christians generally use it to designate, "The congregation of all the faithful, who, being baptized, profess the same doctrine, partake of the same sacraments, and are governed by their lawful pastors, under one visible head on earth." The Church is also called *the body of Christ*, and *the pillar and ground of the truth*. It is the congregation to whom St. Peter addressed the words: "But ye are a chosen generation, a royal priesthood, an holy nation, a peculiar people ; that ye should shew forth the praises of Him who *hath called* you out of darkness into His marvellous light." The Church of Christ, then, is not a voluntary association : it is a divine creation. It was built by Christ Himself. " Upon this rock I will build my Church." Are more words necessary to establish the fact, that the Church of Christ was built by Christ Himself ? The God-Man, who had a full, clear prevision of the whole future, established an institution to do His work, against which, He solemnly declared, the gates of hell shall not prevail. And, if we carefully consult the Testament, we can see that He made the *perfection* of His Church almost His sole concern. Of this society, before His ascension, He was the visible ruler and teacher. But He promised His disciples, that, after His departure, another Person like Himself, another Paraclete, should take up His abode with them. "I will pray the Father, and He shall give you another Comforter (Paraclete), that He may abide with you *forever*; even the Spirit of truth ; whom the world cannot receive, because it seeth him not, neither knoweth him : but ye know him ; for he dwelleth with you, and shall be *in you*." (St. John, XIV. 16, 17.) "When he, the Spirit of truth, is come, he will guide you into all truth : for he shall not speak of himself ; but whatsoever he shall hear, that shall he speak : and he will shew you things to come He shall glorify me : for he shall receive of mine, and shall shew it unto you." (St. John, XVI. 13,14.) On the day of Pentecost, ten days after the Ascension, the Holy Ghost made His visible descent, to dwell in the Church until the end of time. Then the Church, the body of Christ, having received her Spirit, was completed. That the Church, the mystical body of Christ, is pervaded and animated by the Holy Ghost, is fully drawn out by St. Paul. (I. Cor. XII.) The Apostles instilled into their disciples the same truth. " Where the Church is," said

St. Iren., "there is also the Spirit of God; and where the Spirit of God is, there is the Church and all grace."(*Ubi enim Ecclesia, ibi et Spiritus Dei; et ubi Spiritus Dei, illic Ecclesia, et omnis gratia: Spiritus autem veritas. Cont. Hæret. lib. iii. cap. 24.*) "Where these are — that is, the Father, Son, and Holy Ghost —there is the Church, which is the Body of the Three," said Tertullian.(*Quoniam ubi tres, id est Pater et Filius et Spiritus Sanctus, ibi Ecclesia quæ trium corpus est.—De Bapt. sect. vi. ed. Rigalt. p. 226.*) St. Augustine said: "For what the soul is to the body of a man, that the Holy Ghost is to the body of Christ, which is the Church. What the Holy Ghost does in the whole Church, that the soul does in all the members of one body."(*Quod autem est anima corpori hominis, hoc est Spiritus Sanctus corpori Christi, quod est Ecclesia: hoc agit Spiritus Sanctus in tota Ecclesia, quod agit anima in omnibus membris unius corporis. —Sermo in Die Pent. i. tom. v. p. 1090.*) Also: "What our spirit—that is, our soul—is to our members, that the Holy Ghost is to the members of Christ, to the body of Christ, which is the Church." (*Quod est spiritus noster, id est anima nostra, ad membra nostra; hoc Spiritus Sanctus ad membra Christi, ad corpus Christi, quod est Ecclesia. —Sermo in Die Pent. ii. tom. v. p. 1091.*) He said, besides: "Therefore of two is made one person, of the Head and the body, of the bridegroom and the bride. . . . If there are two in one flesh, *how not two in one voice?* Therefore let Christ speak, because in Christ the Church speaks, and in the Church Christ speaks, both the body in the Head and the Head in the body." (*Fit ergo tamquam ex duobus una quædam persona, ex capite et corpore, ex sponso et sponsa. . . Si duo in carne una, cur non duo in voce una? Loquitur ergo Christus, quia in Christo loquitur Ecclesia, et in Ecclesia loquitur Christus; et corpus in capite, et caput in corpore.—In Psal. xxx. tom. iv. p. 147.*) "But now the Holy Ghost," said St. Greg. Naz., "is given more perfectly, for He is no longer present by His *operation* as of old, but is present with us, so to speak, and converses with us in *a substantial manner*."(Orat, XLI. in Pentecost. tom. I. p. 749.) (I have taken these extracts from Cardinal Manning's "Temporal Mission.") To people who hardly ever hear any reference to the Church, this notion of it will be startlingly novel; but it has been taught, from the first, by the profoundest scholars within her pale, and even seems to be coming into vogue with some outside of it. Hugh Miller Thompson, in a little tract called "First Principles," says: "For this kingdom is not only a kingdom. It is not a *mere* polity. It is more than a mere society. This wondrous kingdom is a *living organism*—a body—a living, growing, thinking, feeling, working body." (p. 40.)

As to duration the Church is INDEFECTIBLE. It was predicted; "I will make an everlasting covenant with them. And their seed shall be known among the Gentiles, and their offspring among the people: all that see them shall acknowledge them, that they are the seed which the Lord hath blessed." (Is. LXI. 8, 9.) "In the days of these kings shall the God of heaven set up a kingdom, which shall never be destroyed. . . . and it shall stand forever." (Dan. II. 44.) "God will establish it forever." (Ps. XLVIII. 8.) It was expressly affirmed by our Lord Himself. "On this rock I will build my Church, and the gates of hell shall not prevail against it." "Lo, I am with you *always*, even unto the end of the world." These clear proofs from Scripture should be sufficient for the perpetuity of the Church.

The Church is VISIBLE. By the visibility of the Church is meant her conspicuous existence, her manifest external organization, and her public confession and preaching of the Faith. As her visibility is sometimes denied, proofs numerous and varied may not be needless. "I have set watchmen upon thy walls, O Jerusalem, which shall never hold their peace day nor night: ye that make mention of the Lord, keep not silence." (Is. LXII. 6.) "Yet shall not thy *teachers* be removed into a corner any more, but thine eyes shall see thy teachers." (Is. XXX. 20.) "Ye are the light of the world. A city that is set on an hill cannot be hid." (St. Matt. v. 14.) "I have set thee to be a light of the Gentiles, that thou shouldest be for salvation unto the ends of the earth." (Acts, XIII. 47.) Unless the Church is perceptible, how can the injunction, "Hear the Church," be obeyed? In the 17th chapter of St. John's Gospel, Jesus prays for the unity of His disciples, "that the world may believe that thou, Father, hast sent me." How could the world discern their unity, if it be not visible? The visibility of the Church has been believed in, and taught, by the great majority of Christians. Copious quotations, patristic and modern, could be given, in confirmation of this; but space and time can be saved by making one from the Protestant Palmer. He says: "It would be superfluous to prove that those of the Roman obedience and the Eastern Churches maintain the visibility of the church; none of them have ever denied it. But the perpetual visibility of the church has been also acknowledged by the Lutherans, the Reformed, and by various sects." ("Church," Vol. I. p. 33.) Butler, in his "Analogy," has: "Miraculous powers were given to the first preachers of Christianity, in order to their introducing it into the world; *a visible church* was established, in order to continue it, and carry it on successively throughout all ages. Had Moses and the Prophets, Christ and his Apostles, only taught, and by miracles proved, religion to their contemporaries, the benefits of their instructions would have reached but to a small part of mankind. Christianity must have been, in a great degree, sunk and forgot in a very few ages. To prevent this, appears to have been one reason why a visible church was instituted; to be, like a city upon a hill, a standing memorial to the world of the duty which we owe our Maker; to call men continually, both by example and instruction, to attend to it, and, by the form of religion ever before their eyes, remind them of the reality; to be the repository of the oracles of God; to hold up the light of revelation in aid to that of nature, and propagate it throughout all generations to the end of the world." (p. 140.) The Protestant Kurtz ("Sacred History,"(p. 416.) says: "There is also a distinction made between the visible and the invisible Church. The former is the external union of all those who are baptized in the name of Christ and who confess his name; among these there are many pretended and nominal Christians. The latter, on the contrary, is the communion of all the true and living members of the external church, who confess Christ not only with the mouth, but also with their whole heart. While this distinction is made, the fact ought, under no circumstances, to be overlooked, that the invisible Church has no existence without the visible Church, and that it is not separate from, or above the latter, but exists *in* it, and in it *alone*. For the Means of Grace have been granted, not to the invisible but to the visible Church, and the believer can have part in the grace of God in so far only as he is a member of the visible Church, and by virtue of that connection alone."

"The ultimate reason of the visibility of the Church is to be found in the *incarnation* of the Divine Word. Had that Word descended into the hearts of men, without taking the form of a servant, and accordingly without appearing in a corporeal shape, then only an internal, invisible Church would have been established. But since the Word became *flesh*, it expressed itself in an outward, perceptible, and human manner; it spoke as man to man, and suffered, and worked after the fashion of men, in order to win them to the kingdom of God; so that the means selected for the attainment of this object, fully corresponded to the general method of instruction and education determined by the nature and the wants of man. This decided the nature of those means, whereby the Son of God, even after He had withdrawn himself from the eyes of the world, wished still to work in the world, and for the world. The Deity having manifested its action in Christ according to an *ordinary human fashion*, the form also in which His work was to be continued, was thereby traced out." (Moehler's "Symbolism," p. 253.)

The Church has for her recognition the four notes of UNITY, HOLINESS, CATHOLICITY, and APOSTOLICITY.

The Church is ONE. In organizing a society, to preach the Gospel for all time, the antecedent probability would be, that our Saviour designed its continual integrity; that its members should always be in harmonious accord on all matters that affect the efficiency of their labors. The wisdom of man is sufficient to know the advantages and the power of unanimity. If, however, the Scriptures be consulted, we shall find that the unity of the Church was foretold, and that it was for her unity that Jesus prayed especially. "My dove, my undefiled is but one; she is the only one of her mother, she is the choice one of her that bare her." (S. S. VI. 9.) "They shall call thee, the city of the Lord, the Zion of the Holy One of Israel." (Is. LX. 14.) "And there shall be one fold, and one shepherd." (St. John, X. 16.) "And (that Jesus should die) not for that nation only, but that also He should gather together in *one* the children of God that were scattered abroad." (Id. XI. 52.) "So we, being many, are one body in Christ, and every one members one of another." (Rom. XII. 5.) "There is one Body, and one Spirit, even as ye are called in one hope of your calling: one Lord, *one faith*, one baptism." (Eph. IV. 4, 5.) "For His Body's sake, which is the Church." (Col. I. 24.) "And gave Him to be the Head over all things to the Church, which is His Body, the fullness of Him that filleth all in all." (Eph. I. 22, 23.) And that this unity would always subsist is evident (provided that His prayer would be of any avail) from : "Neither pray I for these alone, but for them also which shall believe on Me through their word ; that they all may be one ; as Thou, Father, art in Me, and I in Thee, that they also may be one in Us: that the world may believe that Thou hast sent Me. And the glory which Thou gavest Me I have given them ; that they may be one, even as We are one." (St. John, XVII. 20-22.) On this passage Mœhler remarks: "What fulness of thoughts we find here! The Lord putteth up a prayer for the gift of unity, and the union of all who shall believe; and for an unity, too, which finds its model only in the relation existing between the Father and the Son of Man." (Sym. p. 266.) To finish this note : As the Holy Ghost abides forever in the mystical Body of Christ, so the Church of Christ, which is His mystical Body, can never be other than *one*.

The Church is HOLY. She derives her holiness from the character of her Founder : she is holy, too, because she is the source of purity and sanctity. "And they shall call them, the holy people, the redeemed of the Lord." (Is. LXII. 12.) "That he might present it to himself a glorious church, not having spot, or wrinkle, or any such thing ; but that it should be holy and without blemish." (Eph. v. 27.) "Who hath saved us, and called us with an holy calling." (II Tim. I. 9.) The holiness of the Church is assured by the abiding presence within her of the Holy Ghost, the Sanctifier.

The Church is CATHOLIC. By the catholicity of the Church is meant that the Church is an institution designed, not for a locality alone, nor for even any particular nation, but for the whole world. The Church of Christ was to be universal. "In the last days, the mountain of the Lord's house shall be established in the top of the mountains, and shall be exalted above the hills : and *all nations* shall flow unto it." (Is. II. 2.) "For from the rising of the sun even unto the going down of the same my name shall be great among the Gentiles ; and in every place incense shall be offered unto my name, and a pure offering : for my name shall be great among the heathen, saith the Lord of hosts." (Mal. I. 11.) As, also, Christ died for all men, instituted but one Church, and commanded his disciples to preach the gospel to all nations, so is it perfectly manifest that His Church was to be Catholic, or Universal. The Church of Christ was also to teach *all* the truth ; teach it *always* ; and teach it *everywhere*. (St. Matt. xxviii. 20.)

The Church is APOSTOLICAL. This attribute of the Church signifies that her accredited ministers are only those who derive their order and mission, by an uninterrupted succession from the Apostles. Under the old law no man could usurp the priest's office. "No man taketh this honour unto himself, but he that is called of God, as was Aaron." (Heb. v. 4.) For foisting themselves into the priesthood Korah, Dathan, and Abiram were swallowed up ; and, if the dignity of the old priesthood was not to be assumed by merely human power, how can the ministry of the Gospel, so much higher in dignity than that of the law, be an heritage purely human ? Christ said to His Apostles, "As my Father hath sent Me, even so send I you." By these words He empowered them to give mission to others, and that this mission was transferable, is shown by His conferring it on them. Those that received mission from the Apostles received with it the power of its transmission, and in this way alone a valid ministry must have been continued. Even Paul, after he was miraculously called, was subjected to the laying on of hands, by "certain prophets and teachers." This was done no doubt to serve as a warning example against the assumption of ministerial functions by a self-constituted prophet. An "inward call," without an external one, is a very thin foundation to ground a mission on. If one be divinely called, it would scarcely be to act in opposition to the laws and discipline of the Church of Christ. But there were to be preachers who "call" themselves. Jesus spoke of the impostor that "came in his own name." (St. John, v. 43.) "And many false prophets shall rise, and shall deceive many." (St. Matt. xxiv. 11.) "The time will come when they will not endure sound doctrine; but after their own lusts shall they heap to themselves teachers, having itching ears; and they shall turn away their ears from the truth, and shall be turned unto fables." (II Tim. iv. 3, 4.) Obviously it concerns us to know well who are our teachers. But, how can we discover or know the true teachers of Christianity? The true and the false meet us with the same declaration of their having been *sent*. There should be no difficulty about the one that stands out alone as a "specialist;" but some that boast of a descent may give more trouble, though after a little examination it will sometimes be discovered, that the boldest of them is "a son without a father, a disciple without a master, and a successor without a predecessor."

The only teachers of Christianity are those that are *sent* by the Church of Christ; and the Church is Apostolical, because the power of transmitting mission belongs to her alone.

The Church (*Ecclesia docens*) is INFALLIBLE. This means that in her teaching she is inerrable, that she does not, can not, teach aught but the truth. She is the "*pillar and ground of the truth.*" Were the Church fallible, she would be an imperfection; but she is the creation of Jesus Christ; she is consequently *perfection*, and so infallible. John said to the Church: "Ye have an unction from the Holy One, and ye know all things. . . . But the anointing which ye have received of him abideth in you, and *ye need not that any man teach you*: but as the same anointing teacheth you of all things, and is truth, and is no lie, and even as it hath taught you, ye shall abide in him."

(II. 20-27.) Christ, too, left the commandment, "*Hear the Church.*" But this He never would have given, unless the Church be unerring in her judgment and distinct in her utterance. He never would have left us subject to a fallible authority. And of the Church's perpetual infallibility we are certain, because the intimate, indwelling union of the Holy Ghost with the Church was promised forever.

I conclude this letter with an extract from the "Temporal Mission."

"As in the Incarnation there is a communication of the Divine perfections to the humanity, so in the Church the perfections of the Holy Spirit become the endowments of the body. It is imperishable, because He is God; indivisibly one, because He is numerically one; holy, because He is the fountain of holiness; infallible, both in believing and in teaching, because His illumination and His voice are immutable, and therefore, being not an individual depending upon the fidelity of a human will, but a body depending only on the Divine will, it is not on trial or probation, but is itself the instrument of probation to mankind. It cannot be affected by the frailty or sins of the human will, any more than the brightness of the firmament by the dimness or the loss of human sight. It can no more be tainted by human sin than the holy sacraments, which are always immutably pure and divine, though all who come to them be impure and faithless. What the Church was in the beginning it is now, and ever shall be in all the plenitude of its divine endowments, because the union between the body and the Spirit is indissoluble, and all the operations of the Spirit in the body are perpetual and absolute."

LETTER X.

THE CHURCH (CONTINUED).

Besides being one, holy, catholic, and apostolical, the Church, endowed with immortality, designed for the regeneration of all nations, and directed in all her movements and solemn utterances by the presiding guidance of the Holy Ghost, must seem, in her bearing and voice towards the world, to be invidiously exclusive and unflinchingly positive. To the world she must always have appeared singular in her constancy to herself, *the pillar and ground of the truth;* and this superior isolation would be a sure warrant, that she is not a kingdom of this world As she was instituted to teach the world and would fully understand herself and her mission, she must always have refused to be instructed by the world; she must have rejected with the firmest decision every proposal of compromise with sentiment or doctrine alien to her own spirit and teaching, and so to the world must always have been an object of envy and hatred. "If ye were of the world, the world would love his own: but because ye are not of the world, but I have chosen you out of the world, therefore the world hateth you." (St. John, xv. 19.) In history, then, a continuous struggle between the Church and the world may be expected to have been, must have been :. envy and hatred waging continual warfare against winning clemency, but stubborn persistence in the truth. Since, too, she would likely, in conformity with Scriptural teaching, reject "a man that is an heretic after the first and second admonition," and hold aloof from "every brother that walketh disorderly, and not after the tradition which he received of us," there would be nothing extraordinary in her having cast from her communion heretical and obstreperous members. These may have clamored against her too. In short, her enemies would be of every kind, of every stripe. Should not all this be carefully borne in mind, when we set out to discover the Church of Christ?

Has there been, from the time of the Apostles to the present, a visible society of Christians, unbroken in its continuity, that has unremittingly striven to keep itself one in faith and government, that has been holy, universal, and apostolical, and which has been branded by the world and empirical Christians, with the stigma (glory) of intolerance? Consult ecclesiastical history, it matters not whose, and you will find, that the Catholic Church, and she alone, has been "the city that is set on a hill:" that has preserved from the first her entirety, her faith, and even discipline; that has been the constant dispenser of Divine graces; that has ramified to every corner of the known world and converted the nations; that has alone been able to use the word apostolical; and that has been envied and hated by all outside of her fold.

The Catholic Church has been a public witness to the truth ever since the time of the Apostles. Can any other body of professing Christians boast of such a long visible existence? It seems surprising, that among Protestants, who rejoice in Luther for a father, there can be found those who assert, that they have a chain of ancestors, that connected Luther to the Apostles! It is one of those absurd statements, begotten entirely of desperation. Even Waddington, to whom every Protestant ought to pay humble homage, destroys it. "In the meantime, we must admit, that he (Bossuet) has, in our opinion, established his two leading positions; viz., that the Protestants fail in their attempts to prove an uninterrupted succession; and that those whom they claim as their ancestors differed from them in numerous points of doctrine." (Ch. Hist., p. 553.) On page 555, he sums up again with: "Upon the whole, then, it seems impossible to establish on historical ground the theory of an uninterrupted transmission of the original faith from the primitive times to those of Luther." (This man is, of course, one of those who hold that the "original faith" became corrupted or lost; in other words, that the Church of Christ was overcome by the gates of hell. Palmer told us, page 62, that such "is a decidedly heretical position." It is worse: *it makes a false prophet of Jesus Christ.* But we may be sure, that, if there were any thing like age for Protestantism, with its face washed or unwashed, Waddington had the inclination and the ability to describe its extent. He cannot, though, go back of Luther.) Show this to a common Protestant and he will say: "Ah, but herein is your error; you assume that the true Church is visible; we contend that the church is the congregation of the saints, the elect, who are known to God alone; and such were our ancestors, pious souls, who, within the recesses of their hallowed breasts, treasured the pure faith, and bemoaned in silence the dissemination of corrupt doctrines which they dared not denounce and combat." Substantially this is what he will say: it is all he can say. But, let me ask, how could such men be Christians? Men who are ashamed or afraid to declare their faith are no soldiers of Christ. Christians were to be "watchmen who should never hold their peace;" the ancient Protestants were seemingly "watchmen who held their peace." According to the representations of their best friends, not one of them stood up to "fight the good fight of faith," nor to "earnestly contend for the faith which was once delivered unto the saints." Neither were they hardy imitators of St. Paul, who said to the Thessalonians: "We were bold in our God to speak unto you the Gospel of God with much contention." "He that taketh not his cross, and followeth after Me, is not worthy of Me. He that findeth his life shall lose it; and he that loseth his life for My sake shall find it." (St. Matt. x. 38, 39.) (For accommodation I quote throughout King James's Bible.) An invisible, independent of a visible, Church, besides being flatly in contradiction to her Scriptural description, is, as a promulgator of the Gospel, an impossibility. To evangelize the world, the faith must be publicly taught by authorized teachers; there must be rites and ceremonies; the sacraments must be administered; and, if all these things be done "decently and in order," there must be laws to which all must submit. The true Church, therefore, can not but be visible. If those Protestants would read the fifth chapter of Mœhler's "Symbolism" and ponder it well, they would never again speak of an invisible, without a visible, Church. They would then see that Luther spoke rightly, when he said, ' At first I stood alone."

Only the Catholic Church has been successful in heeding the behest, " to keep the unity of the Spirit in the bond of peace," and her constant text has been " one body and one Spirit:" her unity has been the reproach cast against her by her enemies; her unchangeableness has passed into a proverb. From the first, detachments have deserted her fold, to set up rival institutions (1 Cor. XI. 19. II Peter, II. 1.); but their success has always been thwarted by divisions upon divisions: she alone has preserved herself in every age and in every place. If history shows any thing, it shows this.

The holiness of the Church may not be so plain to every historical reader. He so often encounters bad characters (generally upon hostile testimony though), who are too often churchmen, that, when he hears holiness applied to the Church, he gets confused. But on this subject Pearson, in his "Creed," p. 523, says: "I conclude, therefore, as the ancient Catholics did against the Donatists, that within the church, in the public profession and external communion thereof, are contained persons truly good and sanctified, and hereafter saved ; and together with them other persons void of all saving grace, and hereafter to be damned : and that church containing these of both kinds may well be called *holy*, as *St. Matthew* called *Jerusalem the holy city*, even at that time when our Saviour did but begin to preach, when we know there was in that city a general corruption in manners and worship." Palmer, " Church," Vol. I. p. 134, says : " It is asserted by some that a society which includes a number of unholy men cannot be a church of Christ, that the true church comprises only saints or perfect Christians, and that sinners cannot be members of it. The Novatians and Donatists considered all who were guilty of great sins as forming no part of the church. The Pelagians held the church to consist only of perfect men free from sin. The Wickliffites taught that the church includes only the predestinate. The Anabaptists and the English dissenters asserted, that it consists only of those who are visibly holy in their lives ; and the latter founded their separation from the church on the principle that she comprised so many sinners in her communion. Therefore they departed from her, to form a pure society of saints in which no sinner was to find place. Their whole system was founded, and continues to be maintained on the fiction that their communities are all holy, pure, perfect saints, incapable of passion, strife, tyranny, &c. Against these principles, which have unhappily been refuted long ago by *experience*, I maintain the following position. . . . ." In the Church there were to be wheat and tares together; and the tares will not only have been multiplied and exaggerated, perhaps, by the enemies of the Church, but must always have been the concern and trouble of the Church herself. But, in reading history, we should mind this : " Sin, in some shape or other, is the great staple of history, and the sole object of law; and he (historical reader) must expect, from both the historian and the legislator, to hear more of one turbulent prelate, or one set of factious or licentious monks, than of a hundred societies, or a thousand scattered clergy, living in the quiet decency suited to their profession." (Maitland's D. A., p. 34.) Westcott says pretty much the same: "Exceptional phenomena naturally occupy a chief place in a history. No one thinks it necessary to chronicle what is the normal state of things." ("Canon," p. xxxiii.) If, however, abundant historical evidence would be acceptable, to show that the Church has never been without the most illustrious characters, who by their virtues have shed a lustre on their times, and who stand out in glorious contrast with the few objectionable ones that figure in the annals of common history, let me recommend (hold your breath) for careful reading Butler's "Lives of the Saints." You cannot come down to it? Possibly not, but Gibbon managed to go through it, called it "a work of merit," and was not above consulting it for information. The "Imperial Dictionary of Biography" says, the work "earned the praise of Bishop Lowth, and even of Gibbon." But, if you would prefer DuPin's "History of Ecclesiastical Writers," translated by a Protestant, try that; or read the "Lives of the Saints," as written by the Protestant Baring-Gould. Then you will find, upon honest consideration, that the Catholic Church is the only church that has reared, to any approximation of perfection, men who can strictly be called saints. As, therefore, the Church has always produced Saints, has instilled holiness of doctrine, has possessed the means of sanctity, and has enforced the obligation of good works, so has she always been holy.

Catholicity, or Universality, has by the world been applied to only one Church, and only one Church has constantly called herself Catholic. Only one Church has taught the same faith, administered the same sacraments, and enforced the same discipline, during nearly nineteen hundred years, in every part of the known world; only one Church has been a mother to all the nations; and the same Church is the same to-day. She is the one, holy, Catholic Church. The word *Catholic* has its attractions. It has been arrogated by various schismatical bodies; but none of them have been able to give it more extension than something national or insignificantly local. St. Augustine observed, in his day, that "all heretics wish to be called Catholics, yet if a stranger ask them, Where is the Catholic Church? not a heretic of them all will dare show you his own church." These robust upstarts, self-called catholics, dub Catholics, "Romanists." It is an old Arian trick. St. Gregory of Tours says, that the Arians, long ago, pointed out the "Romanists:" "*Romanorum nomine vocitant nostræ religionis homines.*" The Paulicians, too, "applied the title of Romans to the Catholics." (Hase, p. 160.) But, what Church is to-day in *every* country of North America, in *every* state of South America, in *every* nation of Europe, in every part of Asia where a European dares put his foot, and in the great islands? There is one and only one: she is the Catholic Church.

The Church that has been one, holy, and catholic, has also been apostolical. There was but one Church built by Christ and established by the Apostles, and the same Church has been throughout controlled and instructed by men that have lineally derived their authority from the Apostles. And the history of the Church shows, that the most scrupulous care has always been observed by her in the selecting of suitable men for the priesthood, and the valid transmission of orders. St. Irenæus said: "We can enumerate those who were by the Apostles instituted bishops in the churches, and their successors even to us." (*Habemus annumerare eos qui ab apostolis instituti sunt episcopi in ecclesiis, et successores eorum usque ad nos.*)

And: "Wherefore it is necessary to obey those presbyters who are in the Church, those who have succession from the Apostles." (*Quapropter eis qui in ecclesia sunt, presbyteris obaudire oportet, his qui successionem habent ab apostolis.*) This was the belief and practice of the Church in the first flush of her onset against the world, as is so distinctly asserted by St. Irenaeus who may be called the grandson of St. John, for he was the disciple of Polycarp who was a disciple of St. John. And the same has been the practice of the Church ever since. In the Church, besides an "inward call," a man must produce to veterans in the ministry evident tokens of moral fitness and intellectual qualifications, and betray some slight diffidence in his own unaided sufficiency, before he can be enrolled with the teachers of Christianity. Elsewhere matters are managed a little differently. "The Reformed held the *call of the people* the only thing essential to the validity of the ministry; and teach, that ordination is only a ceremony, which renders the call more august and authentic." (Watson's Dict., *Ordination*.) Now, it would naturally be expected, that people who go so much upon Scripture would have some Testamentary warrant or example to defend a procedure so foreign to Christian custom. But I am told that Scripture does not countenance any thing of the sort. Palmer, Vol. i. p. 170, quotes the nonconformist James for this: "*No case occurs in the inspired history where it is mentioned that a church elected its pastor.*" Scriptural or unscriptural, however, it would seem to be a visible call, at any rate; but, to be serious, why, according to it, cannot a gang of gipsies give order and mission to a preacher? And when the new lights declared, that "ordination is *only* a ceremony," they avowed a marked difference of belief with the Church. The Church says, as St. Paul told Timothy, that at ordination "a gift" (the grace of order) is bestowed "with the laying on of the hands of the presbytery." Though after all, it is exceedingly probable, that, with the "Reformed," "ordination is *only* a ceremony." But what must be patent to every one, who brings but a modicum of common sense to bear on the subject, is the utter senselessness of setting apart in Protestantism a body of men for Christian teachers. The Bible, which every body can read and *perfectly understand*, contains all that is necessary for salvation. Who, then, wants a teacher? In the conditions, he can be nothing but an expensive intruder. As the sacraments are only empty signs, essential or non-essential, according to the rise or the fall of popular taste, and as the preacher himself, having been the victim of "*only* a ceremony," can have no peculiar power, the question naturally bares itself, why is not a lay baptism or a lay distribution of bread as valid as if either or both were celebrated by a preacher? What effect can *he* add to either sign?

Infallibility must belong to the Church founded by Christ. *His* Church was a *divine* creation, and was to be *divinely* directed—by the Holy Ghost—for all time, and what is *divine* must be infallible. What Church to-day calls herself infallible? There is only one, the Catholic Church. All the other religious bodies have the modesty to disclaim every pretension to inerrancy. They deny the existence of any infallible tribunal. But she, trusting to the promise of Christ, that the Spirit of Truth should abide with her forever, triumphantly keeps up the continuous cry, "I always speak the same words: I am infallible." And the indisputable fact, that history clearly acquits her of any contradictions, may well arouse the inpotent madness of her numerous enemies. A church that scouts the idea of infallibility would hardly be infallible; it would scarcely ridicule its best recommendation to our deference: on the other hand, an infallible Church would certainly know, and be forward to declare, her infallibility.

Is there any probability that salvation can be certainly found outside of the Catholic Church? I think, it was Luther who said, that a single man on an isolated island can obtain salvation without the Church, a priest, or the sacraments. Perhaps he could, but upon a case so extravagantly hypothetical no general rule can safely rest. Mankind in general are not individual possessors of separate islands. St. Cyprian said: "He cannot have God for his father, who has not the Church for his mother." (*Habere jam non potest Deum Patrem, qui Ecclesiam non habet matrem.*) The consequence, too, of holding aloof from the Church is well pointed out by St. Augustine. "But see what ye have to beware of, to watch over, and to fear. In the body of a man it may happen that a member, the hand, the finger, or the foot, may be cut off. Does the soul follow the severed member? While it was in the body it was alive; cut off, its life is lost. So a man is a Christian and a Catholic while he is alive in the body; cut off, he becomes a heretic. The Holy Ghost does not follow the amputated limb." (*Sed videte quid cavetis, videte quid observetis, videte quid timeatis. Contingit ut in corpore humano, immo de corpore aliquod præcidatur membrum, manus, digitus, pes; numquid præcisum sequitur anima? Cum in corpore esset, vivebat: præcisum amittit vitam. Sic et homo Christianus Catholicus est, dum in corpore vivit; præcisus hæreticus factus est, membrum amputatum non sequitur Spiritus.*) He also says: "If you wish to live by the Spirit of Christ, be in the Body of Christ." (*Si vis vivere de spiritu Christi, esto in corpore Christi.*) And Pearson, in his "Creed," has: "The necessity of believing *the Holy Catholic Church*, appeareth first in this, that *Christ* hath appointed it as the only way unto eternal life. We read at the first that *the Lord added to the Church daily such as should be saved;* and what was then daily done, hath been done since continually. *Christ* never appointed two ways to heaven:

nor did he build a church to save some, and make another institution for other men's salvation. . . . . That Church alone which first began at *Jerusalem* on earth, will bring us to the *Jerusalem* in heaven; and that alone began there which always embraceth *the faith once delivered to the saints*. Whatsoever church pretendeth to a new beginning, pretendeth at the same time to a new churchdom, and whatsoever is so new is none." (pp. 530-532.) The Metodist Watson, too, Dict. Art. *Church*, makes the same thing plain by declaring that we must yield obedience to the *Church*. He says: "'Persons who will not hear the church' are to be held as 'heathen men and publicans,' as those who are not members of it; that is, they are to be separated from it, and regarded as of 'the world,' quite out of the range of the above-mentioned relations of Christians to each other, and their correspondent duties; but still, like 'heathen men and publicans' they are to be the objects of pity, and general benevolence." (A very pertinent question is, did John Wesley hear and obey his mother church? What a death blow it is for all the church makers!)

Whether I was a Catholic when I reached this far, I cannot say; but I can say what finally decided me. It was a review of the history of the heresies. Look at them from the first,—the Gnostics, the Montanists, the Novatians, the Donatists, the Arians, the Pelagians, the Nestorians, the Monophysites, the Monothelites, the Vaudois, the Albigenses, and the other tumultuous hordes of the Middle Ages, and all the others down to the present time. What is their history? The history of any one is formally and finally the history of any other. Some one full of himself discovers, that the Church has been in some doctrine quite in error. Having determined to his own satisfaction what is the certain truth, he proposes it to the Church for her acceptance. But the Church is strictly conservative; she objects to tentative measures;

in fact she refuses to be taught! Her obstinacy is too much for him ; he deserts her fold, and with some that he may induce to desert with him and the outsiders that he can allure to his standard, he forms a party and stamps upon it his own name. But he soon finds out, to his mortification, that his disciples are not as docile and submissive as he would desire. One or more of the hardiest ones propose amendments of their own. There is a quarrel in the camp. The quarrel finishes with a division. The quarrels and divisions continue, until at last the particular truth first offered to the Church is believed by nobody. A heresy is nearly always local and short-lived. Who, on looking up the history of the heresies, would say that one of them was right? Who would not say that the man in communion with the Church was in the safe path? The Church, which witnessed their birth, their ephemeral success, and their dying struggles, has pursued her own even course through them all, without the slightest change in her teaching. In what respect did Luther differ from Arius or any other heretic? The two were formally the same. I saw at last, that the churches of the "Reformation" were as purely heretical as the churches of the various forms of Arianism. The Catholic Church is the only Church that can live in every time and every place. As she is the mystical Body, inhabited by the Holy Ghost, she is THE PILLAR AND GROUND OF THE TRUTH, and she can withstand all opposition, all assaults. Here I whispered to myself, "I am a Catholic."

LETTER XI.

RULE OF FAITH.

When the "Reformers" discovered, that the Church taught some doctrines that are nothing but "human opinions," they could not conscientiously remain in her fold any longer. An inspired loathing of every thing human eminently characterized them. After having withdrawn themselves from a corrupt Church and publicly accused her of erroneous teaching, it would be very natural to expect, that such proficients in Christian knowledge would adopt for themselves some rule of faith that would be rational and certain. They took for their primary dogma, that the Written Word *alone* is the complete revelation of divine truth, containing all that a Christian need believe or regard. And this statement, so far from being a respectable "human opinion," hardly rises to the dignity of a decent conjecture. For the Bible, or more particularly perhaps, the Testament, the Protestant professes the highest veneration. This, the Catholic, whose veneration for it is, if any thing, still greater, cannot but approve and admire; but, when the Protestant insists that the Testament was given by God for every man to learn and judge for himself the doctrines of Christianity, the Catholic takes issue with him at once.

It is likely, that, if our Saviour intended that mankind should learn His religion from a book, He Himself would have written all or a part of it, or at the very least would have commanded His Apostles to write it; and in the book somewhere its aim and purpose would be distinctly declared. Not a verse of the Testament did He write, nor is there any evidence that He enjoined His Apostles to write a sentence. And what passage can be selected from the Testament to prove, that it is a full and formal treatise of Christianity? Several can be adduced to show that it is nothing of the kind. St. John said: "And there are also many other things which Jesus did, the which, if they should be written everyone, I suppose that even the world itself could not contain the books that should be written." The fair inference from this, hyperbolical as it may be, is, that all of His instructions to His followers is not in the Testament. It will hardly be said that our Saviour while on earth spoke idle, meaningless words, or did purposeless acts. The Testament, then, to be full and sufficient, should be a complete report. But, according to St. John, it is not.

Had Jesus intended, that from a book alone His religion should be learned, *He* would have given us a book, a plain, solid book, adapted to the lowest capacities; it would contain *all* His teachings, a creed would be formulated in the precisest terms, there would be full and clear instructions concerning the sacraments and their administration, some advice as to its publication and management, and no doubt an ecclesiastical polity expressed in the plainest language: it would not have been a body of fragmentary essays, one containing repetitions of another, and many having "things hard to be understood." But by means of a book alone Christianity would not have made much progress in the world. Since the time of Christ but a small fraction of mankind have been able to read; and for those who could read, before the invention of printing, there were not nor could not be books enough. How could the heathen be converted to-day by the mere agency of a book? Let the Protestants, who have tried it thoroughly, say what their success has been.

For more than three centuries the Protestants have been exclaiming "the Bible and the Bible alone," and with "the Bible alone" they have demonstrated its complete insufficiency. With it their best men have tried to construct a sound theology; and in the attempts their best men have always failed. They have always overlooked or ignored some texts contradictory to their systems, which, in the private opinions of their disciples, have called for vexatious amendments or an entire reconstruction. And the theologians have condescended so often and so completely to the monitions of those whom they have professed to teach, they have so haggled and distorted Scripture to save themselves or to satisfy their people, that they have destroyed authority, stamped out faith, and reduced the truths of Scripture to questions of pure speculation. If the Testament were ever designed for a book wherein men can learn for a certainty all the Christian truths, it has been useless to Protestants. And the truth of this is to be seen not only in the variations of Protestantism in the past, but is to-day abundantly exemplified in the multitudinous divisions, bitter bickerings, and irrepressible jealousies, of those who exercise in vain their private judgments, to discover the fixed sense of the inspired writings. In the Testament man's private judgment perceives very opposite doctrines. The Unitarian lavishes his pity upon the Trinitarian, who claims to be as sincere and just as discriminative as himself; the Episcopalian strives to no purpose against the Presbyterian, to show that episcopacy is a literal injunction; the Calvinist sees all things clustering around grace, and wreaks his indignation upon the simple minded Arminian, who wishes to find room somewhere for free-will; the Baptist makes every thing right by plunging deep into the water, while the Quaker is safer and happier by keeping as far from the water as possible; and the Methodist, who presents himself as a well bleached example of sinless perfection, as little dreads the fire of hell as the Universalist, who is certain that a merciful God would on no account consign a man to everlasting tortures. But what a labor it would be to notice all the differences that divide the hundreds of the Protestant sects! Yet they all declare, that it is from the Bible alone that God expects a man to learn the Christian religion. They lay in great store for themselves, too, for preserving the Scriptures in their first purity! To hear them talk one might suppose that sometime in the misty past a 12mo copy of the Testament was published and bound in heaven, and handed down for Protestant guardianship and interpretation: but there is no positive evidence that Almighty God ever conferred upon Protestantism such a substantial acknowledgment of His countenance; or ever intended, what is contrary "to fact and to faith," that Christianity must be taken from the Bible alone.

If history teaches any thing, it is, that God became man, that He founded a Church, gave her members oral instructions, and commanded them to teach others, *orally*. "And He commanded us to preach unto the people." "He sent them to preach the kingdom of God, and to heal the sick," and to them He declared, "and, lo, I am with you *always, even unto the end of the world*." He never said a word to them about distributing bibles. This may seem to the Protestant to have been a sad misconception of the proper means to the object in view, the Christianizing of the nations; but the *facts* stand on record. Still, by observing to the letter the commands of their Master, the Apostles, we have every reason to believe, met with considerable success. They preached, and, without circulating even a tract, they established Christianity. From the Ascension, A. D. 30, to A. D. 41, when, according to the Methodist commentator, Benson, St. Matthew wrote his Gospel, there was not a sentence of the New Testament written. For eleven years the Church alone was manifest to the world, doing her work fully, and never more successfully. During that time, unless a Protestant, had he then existed, would "hear the Church," he would, without "the Book," have been lonely indeed. What could he have done? It would be a vicious reflection on his enlightened good sense to suppose, that he would have taken the bare statements of the Apo tles, without being allowed the privilege of testing things by his own ideas of what ought to be, or what ought not to be. They would have required his submission to their corporate authority; he would have referred every thing to himself. Their simple allegation, that in their teachings they were specially aided by the Holy Ghost, he would have met with either an incredulous snort, or a counter-claim of his own to still higher pretensions. In A. D. 41, he could have used against them St. Matthew's Gospel, provided he could read Hebrew (Syro-Chaldaic), though five or six years afterwards it would have been easier for him in his favorite Greek. In A. D. 65, he could have reinforced himself with St. Mark's Gospel, and a little afterwards with St. Luke's. And from that time onward he would have found himself overwhelmed with Gospels. Besides the Gospels and Epistles that now make the Testament, he would have encountered (See DuPin) The Letter of Jesus Christ to Agbarus, The Letters of the Virgin Mary, The Gospel according to the Egyptians, The Gospel according to the Hebrews, The *Proto-Evangelion* of St. James, The Epistle to the Laodiceans, The Letters of St. Paul to Seneca, The Epistle of St. Barnabas (the Apostle), The Liturgies of St. Peter—of St. Mark—of St. James—and of St. Matthew, The Canons and Constitutions of the Apostles, The Book of Phochorus, The Ancient Acts of the Passion of St. Andrew, and many, many other writings that were put afloat by the early heretics. How could he have discriminated from such a host of writings the inspired books?

Who did so? And when was it done? Westcott, in "Canon of the New Testament," says: "The formation

of the Canon was an act of the intuition of the Church."
(p. 57.) "It is then to the Church, as 'a witness and
keeper of holy writ,' that we must look both for the formation and the proof of the Canon." (Id. p. 12.) The Lutheran Kurtz, in "Sacred History," says: "The Canon
of the New Testament, as it is now recognized, was settled, and received the sanction of the Church at the
Council of Hippo Regius (Africa), A. D. 393." (p. 405.)
(And Westcott, in 'Canon,' p. 440, speaking of this
Council, says, that Tobit and "two books of the Maccabees" were included with "the canonical Scriptures.")
Mosheim has: "The opinions, or rather the conjectures
of the learned, concerning the time when the books of the
New Testament were collected into one volume, as also
about the authors of that collection, are extremely different. This important question is attended with great and
almost insuperable difficulties to us in these latter times."
(Ch. Hist., Vol. I. p. 108.) On the next page, he says:
"For, not long after Christ's ascension into heaven, several histories of his life and doctrines, full of pious frauds
and fabulous wonders, were composed by persons whose
intentions, perhaps, were not bad, but whose writings
discovered the greatest superstition and ignorance. Nor
was this all: productions appeared which were imposed
upon the world by fraudulent men, as the writings of the
holy apostles. These apocryphal and spurious writings
must have produced a sad confusion, and rendered both
the history and the doctrine of Christ uncertain, had not
the rulers of the church used all possible care and diligence in separating the books that were truly apostolical
and divine from all that spurious trash, and conveying
them down to posterity in one volume." Westcott, says:
"It cannot however be denied that the idea of the Inspiration of the New Testament, in the sense in which it is
maintained now, was the growth of time."('Canon,' p. 55.)
On page 56, he says: "The successors of the Apostles did

not, we admit, recognize that the written histories of the Lord and the scattered epistles of His first disciples would form a sure and sufficient source and test of doctrine."

It is plain now, that the Church was doing perfect work, before a word of the Testament was written; that the books of the Testament were written, as occasion or necessity required them, by members of the Church, and inspired by the Holy Ghost, the Spirit of the Church. *The Testament, then, was made by the Church.* So, only in the Church where the Spirit presides, that inspired and dictated the Scriptures, can their use and import be surely known. From the first, too, the Church has carefully preserved the Scriptures. Who, then, but the Church can give all the necessary vouchers for the Written Word? And, be it observed, unless a Protestant concede a divine judgment to the Church, he can in no way know that the Testament is inspired; since nothing less than a divine judgment, even in forming the Canon, could have distinguished the divine from the human. Hence, by the Church the Scriptures are proved. And by the Scriptures the Church is proved? Not necessarily.

When the Protestant pretends to oppose the Bible to the Church, the Catholic, who is conscious that he can draw abundant proofs from the Scriptures to establish his position, is willing to meet the Protestant on his own ground. And it is only against those who acknowledge the Testament to be the Word of God that he uses Scripture. By other, and quite independent, proofs he can recommend the Church. He can show, for instance, by authentic history, that the Church was established by miracles, that the miracles prove the divine commission, and the divine commission proves the infallibility.(Brownson.) And to prove her unbroken continuity and the divine aid always given her, by which alone she could have maintained herself, he can produce an unbroken chain of evidence from the multitudes of her saints and other writers, that reaches from St. Ignatius to Pope Pius IX. Her present existence will hardly be questioned! Prove the establishment and uninterrupted being of the one, holy, catholic, and apostolic Church! The man that asks for any thing of the kind must be blind to the past.

Concerning the New Testament, it would seem, that for Catholics there is not quite enough in it, and that for Protestants it contains far too much. As the Church ante-dates it, and as it is really nothing but a collection of writings, one epistle addressed to one congregation and another to another, for some purpose dictated by the necessity of the occasion, it is easy to understand, that the Church may have had practices and even beliefs, not mentioned nor noticed in any one of the fugitive, though inspired, writings. Why should we expect to find in letters of counsel and exhortation, addressed to people established in the faith by the preaching of the Apostles, particular mention made of what all well knew? But, by implication and by clear, open statements, there is a good deal more in these writings than any Protestant system can cover. Protestants do not need " Hear the Church." "Thou art Peter, and upon this rock I will build my Church," and the precedence always given to Peter, have no significance in Protestantism? The exhortations to unity have no meaning for Protestants; they are ideals of the impossible, to be explained away. " Whosesoever sins ye remit, they are remitted unto them; and whosesoever sins ye retain, they are retained," can find no place in Protestantism. " Is any sick among you? let him call for the elders of the church; and let them pray over him, *anointing him with oil* in the name of the Lord," is very silently passed over. " By which also he went and preached unto the spirits in prison," is used to bolster up no doctrine, nor repeated to lull to devotion: it is simply useless. "Henceforth all generations shall call me blessed," was spoken by "the mother of my Lord," but Protestants are too scripturally enlightened to use either expression. "It is a shame for women to speak in the church," has been practically denied. The benefit of fasting, so often inculcated by counsel and example, has been more scientifically evaded: fasting has been swollen into feasting, an orthographical touch. "This is my body," provokes general indignation. "Obey them that have the rule over you, and submit yourselves, etc.," is null and void; since obedience will scarcely be rendered where no authority can be asserted. The bitter word *heresy*, although catalogued with the most heinous sins, is seldom if ever defined; nor are the bulk of Protestants regularly cautioned against the wiles of those who are "tossed about by every wind of doctrine."

LETTER XII.

PRIMACY OF ST. PETER.

It would be superfluous to point out, what no one will deny, that for every society there must be a government. "No society," says Guizot, "can exist a week, no, not even an hour, without a government." (The Methodist Watson, Dict., Art. *Church*, says, "it may be sufficient generally to observe, that the church of Christ being a visible and permanent society, bound to observe certain rites, and to obey certain rules, the existence of government in it is necessarily supposed.") And I think, that the great bulk of professing Christians are perfectly agreed that our Lawgiver, for the government of His Kingdom, created offices and appointed officers. But, concerning the number and the nature of these offices, there have been interminable discussions. The Presbyterians, comparatively few and quite modern, but sturdy sticklers for their own narrow sense of Scripture, hold up against the hierarchy, composed of the three orders of the episcopate, the priesthood, and the diaconate, the novel system, that officially all the ministers of the Gospel were originally, and should be now, equals; that the two words in the Testament, translated bishop and presbyter, are interchangeable names for the same commissioned teacher and ruler, and that a deacon stands no higher than a lay official, to be used for a few menial duties. To maintain their position, they draw their shaky proofs exclusively from Scripture, innocently oblivious of the simple facts, that the whole matter must have been settled before a word of the Testament was written, and that the Testament neither professes, nor can be reasonably expected, to contain express and decided proofs of the question: they calmly ignore the earliest historical evidence that stands against them, and bare to view the inference, that the Kingdom of Christ had been ignorant of its proper government, before they themselves sprang into existence, in the sixteenth century! St. Ignatius, without doubt a disciple of St. John, and bishop of Antioch, in his epistles, reiterates the command, to obey the bishop, the presbyter, and the deacon. "*And again*, I cried, therefore, with the voice, being among you, and I spake with a loud voice, with the voice of God attend to the Bishop, and the Presbyters, and the Deacons. And there are some who imagine respecting me, that I have said these things as though I knew the divisions of some—but He in whom I am bound is witness to us, that I have not learned these things from men; but the Spirit cried and said these things: 'Without the bishop do nothing.'" (Ep. to Phil., Ch. VII. Cureton's Ig.) His epistles bristle with the names of the three orders. No recension can be found without them. This Hase admits: "The recently discovered Syriac version of his epistles, and especially of his epistle to the Ephesians, presents us with a much more concise, but a no less hierarchical text." (Ch. Hist., p. 73.) The Presbyterians can do nothing with these memorials of St. Ignatius but to pronounce them forgeries. Professor Calvin E. Stowe, whom any Presbyterian might generally take for a backer, says, in his " Origin and History of the Books of the Bible : " " These seven epistles (of St. Ignatius) have been known and read in the Christian churches from the very earliest period. There is an edition of them of about the sixth century, which undoubtedly contains many interpolations ; but the earlier and briefer recensions, of which Archbishop Usher had a Latin translation and J. Voss, the Greek original, may safely be received as genuine throughout." (p. 122.) If Bishops and Presbyters were in all things identical, how is it that Eusebius has preserved catalogues of the successive Bishops of Rome, of Alexandria, of Antioch, of Jerusalem, etc. ? Why, if all were equal, should a succession of individuals, from the very beginning of these churches, stand out so prominently ? On no supposition, except of official authority, can it be accounted for. I once read a Presbyterian effusion, in which it was gravely asserted that episcopacy was invented by St. Cyprian ! Guizot could hardly be expected to make a full, episcopal declaration, but what he says is dead against the Presbyterian theory. " But the moment this society (Church) began to advance, and almost at its birth, for we find traces of them in its earliest documents, there gradually became moulded a form of doctrine, rules of discipline, a body of magistrates: of magistrates called *presbuteroi*, or elders, who afterwards became priests ; of *episcopoi*, inspectors or overseers, who became bishops ; and of *diakonoi*, or deacons, whose office was the care of the poor and the distribution of alms." (History of Civ., p. 37.) Mosheim (Vol. I. p. 180.), speaking of the second century, says : " The *bishops* considered themselves as invested with a rank and character similar to those of the *high-priest* among the Jews, while the *presbyters* represented the priests, and the *deacons* the *Levites.*" Gibbon says: "*Nulla Ecclesia sine Episcopo*, has been a fact as well as a maxim since the time of Tertullian and Irenaeus." (Hist. Vol. I. p. 557.) Alzog (Ch. Hist., Vol. I. p. 200.) says: "The *uniform organization* of all the churches established wherever Christianity spread is an irrefragable proof that the episcopate is of *divine institution*, and the more so as we never hear that the *presbyters* appealed to their ancient constitution against *episcopal rule.*" Palmer very well observes: "How is it possible indeed to suppose that such a pre-eminence could have prevailed universally in the second century without any objection, if it had not been instituted by the Apostles? We know the disturbances which arose in the Church on the time of keeping Easter: how improbable is it, that episcopacy could have been introduced into all churches by merely human authority, without exciting opposition in some quarter.' ("Church," Vol. II. p. 383.) This will always stand against Presbyterianism. If Christ or the Apostles instituted Presbyterianism, which was so soon and so suddenly subverted, where can the history of the subversion be found? The ambitious would have struggled for the highest offices; the disappointed would have vented their mortification. It would have been one of the greatest disturbances connected with the history of the Church; and yet, in all the ancient records, there is not a word about a disturbance of the kind. The common-sense inference would be, then, that Presbyterianism was born, to be known, in the sixteenth century; and that the Anglicans, Greeks, and Catholics are, in this respect and so far, in well informed agreement.

But here the Anglicans strangely rest themselves: they contend, that in the Apostolic college *every* apostle was in all things equal to each of the others; that in jurisdiction all were equals. Accordingly, the Church seems to have been provided, for her highest grade of rulers, with an exalted body of Presbyters!

The Catechism of Trent says: "The Church has, also, but one ruler and one governor, the invisible one, Christ, whom the Eternal Father 'hath made head over all the Church, which is his body;' the visible one, him, who, as legitimate successor of Peter the prince of the Apostles, fills the apostolic chair." Catholics teach, that, *to ensure the unity of the Church and her harmonious action*, Christ clothed one of the Apostles with supreme authority, which authority was to be and has been exercised by his successors. In a general way, they observe, that unity finds its complement in *one*, and that the Church, *a visible body*, must have, for her perfect realization, *a visible head*. They say, too, that for a sheep-fold there must be a shepherd; and for a kingdom a king. To this Mr. Palmer objects, that "many States have subsisted without a monarchy." This is to forget that the Church is a kingdom; and the ruler of a kingdom, or a part of it, is always a king or a viceroy. They say, besides, that, since under the old law the authority of the High Priest was supreme over the Priests and the Levites, and that the synagogue was the type (1 Cor. x. 11.) of the Christian Church, the Church, if modelled after the Mosaic dispensation, can not be without a visible ruler. And that the polity of the synagogue was transferred to the Church is pretty plain from: "But this is not all; for the times of the 'offerings and services' of Christians are referred to the authority of the Lord Himself, who 'commanded that they should not be made at random, or in a disorderly manner, but at fixed seasons and hours.' It is possible that this is only a transference of the laws of the Jewish synagogue, which were sanctioned by the observance of our Saviour, to the Christian Church; as is indeed made probable by the parallel which Clement institutes between the Levitical and Christian priesthood." (Westcott's 'Canon,' p. 27.) Hase also (Ch. Hist., p. 38.), speaking of the appointment of rulers in the early Church, says, they were chosen "after the model of the synagogue." If, too, as Kurtz says, the Church is "a school in which men are divinely educated for salvation," it must, like every other educational institution, be directed and governed by a single head.

But for the pre-eminence of one Apostle there are clear, Scriptural proofs. Scripture may, or may not, make episcopacy plain: it makes nothing plainer than the primacy of St. Peter. However the names of the Apostles are given, Peter, "*the first*," always has, by its position, a marked prominence. He is most emphatically "THE FIRST." It has been accounted for on the choice of suppositions, that he was the eldest of the Apostles, or that he was the first called. Both conjectures are most certainly at variance with facts. If precedence of name be observed to designate the oldest, then was Andrew older than Peter, for we read (St. John, I. 44.) "the city of Andrew and Peter;" and we are told in the same chapter, that Andrew "first findeth his own brother Simon, and saith unto him, We have found the Messias." "And he brought him to Jesus. And when Jesus beheld him, He said, Thou art Simon the son of Jona: *thou* shalt be called Cephas, which is by interpretation, a stone." (Rock) Here, our Lord, for a reason not yet declared, so distinguished one, that *He promised him a new name* by which he was henceforth to be known. It was no mere epithet, like the "sons of thunder," but a special appellation. And, when He ordained the twelve, He formally conferred the name —" And Simon He surnamed Peter." (St. Mark, III. 16.) To Simon alone was a new name given. It had been usual with the Almighty, in ushering in a new dispensation, to confer upon its chief a new name, indicative of the office he was to fill: Abram became Abraham; and Jacob, Israel. Hence, Simon's new name, Peter, a Rock, must have foretokened something important. Foretokened! Its significance is all but open and declared. Simon received a name that belonged to Christ Himself. Christ Himself was the Rock; but, as if to adopt Simon completely and to mark him for His own representative, *He gave him His own name.*

But Jesus made every thing plain (St. Matt. 16-19.) by divulging His reason for calling Simon, The Rock. When He asked His Apostles, "Whom say ye that I am?" Simon answered, "Thou art the Christ, the Son of the living God." For this prompt confession, Jesus said to him, "Blessed art thou, Simon Barjona, for flesh and blood hath not revealed it unto thee, but my Father who is in heaven." With Simon's reply Jesus was evidently well pleased; and what could be more natural than a great and special instance of rewarding such a confession. Jesus said to him: "I say also unto thee, That *thou* art Peter, and upon this rock I will build my church; and the gates of hell shall not prevail against it. And I will give unto *thee* the keys of the kingdom of heaven: and whatsoever thou shalt bind on earth shall be bound in heaven: and whatsoever thou shalt loose on earth shall be loosed in heaven." This is as the Protestant Testament gives it; and, as it stands, it ought to be plain enough. But some of those exegetists, who have beaten their way so triumphantly through most of the prophecies, read it thus: "Thou art Peter, and upon this rock (Myself) I will build my church." Such a reading, though, makes Jesus use the mixed metaphor. *He* would not in the same breath call Himself both the builder and the foundation. But the text can be put into a form so sharp that it will defy all carping. The language used by Christ was the Syro-Chaldaic, at that time the vernacular of Judea. He said: "*Thou art Cepho, and on this Cepho I will build My Church.*" How is this gainsaid?

Some thrust it aside, by denying that Syro-Chaldaic was the language used. If, as it seems, this is their only chance to evade it, they are in a bad difficulty. The Methodist Benson, in Introduction to St. Matthew's Gospel, says: "But it (language) was what Jerome very properly calls Syro-Chaldaic, having an affinity to both the Syrian and Chaldean language, though much more to the latter than the former." Westcott says: "There can be no doubt that the so-called Syro-Chaldaic (Aramæan) was the vernacular language of the Jews of Palestine in the time of our Lord, however much it may have been superseded by Greek in the common business of life. It was in this dialect, the 'Hebrew' of the New Testament, that the Gospel of St. Matthew was originally written." ('Canon,' p. 236.) "It is *exact* in Syro-Chaldaic, the language in which it was spoken by Jesus Christ. Peter was called Cephas; and the word Cepha signifies base, foundation, rock." (Guizot's note on p. 561, Vol. I., of Gibbon's Hist.) Hence, by saying, "*Thou art Cepho, and on this Cepho I will build my Church*," our Lord, beyond all dispute, chose St. Peter for the Foundation on which He would build His Church. No declaration in the Testament is more emphatic. When He would build it, He did not say: it would be "known hereafter." But He declared, that against the Church so built the gates of hell should not prevail. Is it purely "Papistical" to say that the Church was built on Peter?· Hear the Protestant Pearson: "Then was there a Church (and that built upon Peter, according to our Saviour's promise), ..." ("Creed," p. 511.) Bishop Kenrick, on "The Primacy," cites several other eminent Protestants who have made the same flat admission.

To St. Peter were also given the keys and the commission "to bind and to loose;" and, although the power, "to bind and to loose," was afterwards given to the other Apostles, there was surely some deep import in the fact that it was *first* given to him who was to be the only bearer of the keys. The keys were given to St. Peter alone, to him who was alone the foundation of the Church. The holder of the keys, which are the badge of supreme authority, must have a pre-eminent power of binding and loosing. Could greater or more enduring offices be conferred upon him? As in the Church the duties of binding and loosing must always exist, so long must exist the bearer of the keys, St. Peter; and, as no superstructure can outlast its foundation, so the Church must always rest on St. Peter. St. Peter, then, always lives in his successor. Was Christ a true prophet, or not? The question obtrudes itself. Was Christ a true prophet, or not? If he was, there must be to-day a Church that claims St. Peter for her foundation, and the wielder of her keys must be St. Peter's successor. Unless these things be, the Testament is no better than a romance. Moreover, that St. Peter was *the* representative of the collective Apostolate is quite manifest from (St. Luke, XXII. 31-32.): "And the Lord said, Simon, Simon, behold, Satan hath desired to have *you*, that he may sift you as wheat: But I have prayed for *thee*, that *thy* faith fail not: and when thou art converted, strengthen thy brethren." A prayer offered for St. Peter sufficed for all. On him all the others depended. *He was the foundation of the Church.* In the last chapter of St. John's Gospel, we can read that Jesus committed to the care of St. Peter the lambs and the sheep—the laity and the clergy—and he was strictly charged to "feed" all. The whole sheepfold was put under his rule and care. So, St. Peter, "the first," was made the foundation of the Church; he was the sole recipient of the keys; for him alone Jesus prayed; and under his guardianship Jesus put His entire flock. And yet there are some men, scholars and believers by profession, who can see nothing in all this but a little personal honor, of no consequence whatever, that was shown to St. Peter. Mr. Palmer, when arguing against the Presbyterians, very well says: "Indeed *offices chiefly honorary*, would have been inconsistent with the characters and views of Christians in those times." ('Church,' Vol. II. p. 391.) On page 479, Vol. II., he can not learn, from Catholic tradition, "the reasons for which St. Peter had *a personal pre-eminence of honor among the Apostles.*" So must a principle be forgotten and blindness be confessed, to distort the palpable truth.

After the Ascension, St. Peter acted on his commission as Primate. He led the other apostles: they followed him. It is clearly narrated in the Acts of the Apostles. Watson, Dict., says: "Yet an attentive reader of the Acts of the Apostles cannot fail to perceive that upon almost every occasion of difficulty St. Peter is exhibited to our view as standing foremost in the rank of apostles."

No historical fact is better authenticated than that St. Peter established his chair in Rome, and suffered martyrdom there. Of course, it has been denied; but what has not been denied? Eusebius, in his Ch. Hist. p. 52., says: "For immediately under the reign of Claudius (A. D. 42 54.), by the benign and gracious providence of God, Peter, that powerful and great apostle, ... was conducted to Rome against this pest of mankind." On the next page, he says: "The same author (Philo), in the reign of Claudius, is also said to have had familiar conversation with Peter at Rome, whilst he was proclaiming the gospel to the inhabitants of that city." Once more: "Linus, whom he (St. Paul) has mentioned in his Second Epistle to Timothy as his companion at Rome, has been before shown to have been the first after Peter, that obtained the episcopate at Rome." (p. 74.—Bohn's Library.) Of Eusebius, the Father of Church History, who was Bishop of Cæsarea, and died A. D. 340, DuPin says: "Eusebius was one of the most learned men of all antiquity, as both his friends and enemies do equally acknowledge. ... he seems to have been very impartial, very sincere, and a great lover of peace, truth and religion." These positive statements of Eusebius, then, ought to silence for all time those people, who, on no terms, will allow St. Peter to give Rome one visit. But there is more on the subject.

"St. Peter and St. Paul suffered at Rome about A. D. 66, or 67."(Watson's Dict., Art. *Miracles.*)

"St. Peter and St. Paul both suffered at Rome in the First Persecution under Nero, and most likely on the same day, A. D. 67."(Blunt's Key to Ch. Hist., p. 43.)

"Now it on all hands agreed that St. Peter came out of the East to Rome, etc.,"(Collier's Hist., Vol. I. p. 12.)

"The Roman church was particularly honoured, as *having been presided over* by Peter, the first of the apostles, and was, therefore, by many of the fathers, called the see of Peter."(Palmer's 'Church,' Vol. II. p. 499.) On page 501., same volume, he has: "Hence we may see the reason for which the bishops of Rome were styled SUCCESSORS OF ST. PETER by some of the fathers. They were bishops of the particular church which St. Peter had assisted in founding, and over which he had presided: and they were also, as bishops of the principal church, the *most eminent* among the successors of the apostles; even as St. Peter had possessed the preeminence among the apostles themselves."

"Peter could hardly have passed through any see, without leaving behind him some inheritance of peculiar dignity; while Rome, as the scene of his permanent residence and martyrdom, claimed the undoubted succession to almost monarchical supremacy."(Milman's Latin C. I. 143.)

St. Peter was succeeded by Linus, Linus by Anacletus, Anacletus by St. Clement, etc., without a break (see p. 63.), down to Pope Leo XIII., who now fills St. Peter's chair. While in the sees of Antioch, Jerusalem, Alexandria, and Constantinople, the successions have been broken up, suppressed, or obscured by long voids, the

Roman See *alone* has preserved an uninterrupted succession in its episcopate. And how the Roman bishops, who have always called themselves "Successors of Saint Peter," have from the first asserted their right, as Saint Peter's successors, to supreme authority in the government of the Church, and how their claims have been allowed and submitted to by the most prominent ecclesiastics, are matters of Church History.

The first particular exercise of Papal authority was St. Clement's calming the commotions that arose in the Church at Corinth, at the end of the first century. At the time of the disturbance, St. John, the only survivor of the Twelve, was living at Ephesus: St. Clement was bishop of Rome. St. John was next door to Corinth, and St. Clement was away off at Rome; but he, *occupying St. Peter's chair*, interfered in the disturbance. This is a hard case for an opponent of the Papacy: he can neither dispute the facts, nor explain them. During the Paschal controversy, Pope Victor instructed Polycrates, bishop of Ephesus, to convoke a local council, to bring about a uniformity in the observance of Easter. The Asiatics, attempting to defend their custom and showing an inclination to persist in it, were threatened by Victor with excommunication. St. Irenæus gently remonstrated with Pope Victor in their favor, and perhaps prevented the excommunication. If the Pope had no right to do so, surely St. Irenæus would have left something delicious for Mr. Palmer. But I can not stay to particularize all the instances of Papal supremacy, that were exercised in early times. I will satisfy myself by observing, that, whenever the Papal interference has been necessary, the reigning pontiff has never forgotten the duty of his office. In all general councils he has presided, either in person or by his legates; and his countenance has been courted by all. Let me sustain myself with a Protestant quotation. "But Rome was the only see which could claim to be apostolic, and was almost the only medium of ecclesiastical connection with the East. The high reputation which it possessed with respect to apostolical traditions, was so successfully and dispassionately u ed in the controversies of the East, that the party which had the favor of Rome might generally be sure of ultimate victory. Hence, her opinion and her decision as a mediator was continually sought for and as readily given. And even when her interference was disregarded, as in the case of Chrysostom, it was always in behalf of humanity and the people." (Hase's Ch. Hist., p. 142.) Also this: "In fact we find that the Roman church was zealous to maintain the true faith from the earliest period; condemning and expelling the Gnostics, Artemonites, &c. And during the Arian mania, it was the bulwark of the catholic faith." (Palmer's 'Church,' Vol. II. p. 499.)

Of course, the pope has been opposed: what ruler in this world has not been? All, no doubt more, of these recorded oppositions, invariably the outbursts of passion, have been bunched, labelled, and distributed. But what do they prove? Nothing more nor less than this, that opposition to, or defiance of, authority invalidates that authority!

Perhaps no one in early times used more passionate expressions against a pope than did Firmilian of Cæsarea, who sided with St. Cyprian in contending against the validity of heretical baptism; but, as far as I have been able to find out, Protestant scholarship has not unearthed any thing from either Firmilian or St. Cyprian, that brought into question Pope Stephen's authority. Before the time of Luther there seems to have been a sad dearth of "Barrows."

I would like to transcribe a good list of acknowledgments, made by the early and great ecclesiastical writers, in favor of St. Peter and his successors, but I must content myself with a very few.

Almost every body has read the famous sentence of St. Irenaeus (ob. A. D. 202.), bishop of Lyons, in which he so earnestly enjoins communion with St. Peter's See. "Since," he says, "it would be a long task, in such a volume as this, to enumerate the successions of all the churches, therefore, by giving the tradition of that Church, which is the greatest, most ancient, and best known of all—the Church, I mean, which was founded and constituted at Rome by the two most glorious apostles, Peter and Paul, and by declaring the faith, which it announces to mankind, and which comes through the successions of bishops even to our days, we confound all those, who in whatever way, whether from self-conceit, vain glory, or blindness and ill judgment, separate themselves from the body. For to this Church by reason of its superior principality, must every church resort (*Ad hanc enim Ecclesiam propter potentiorem principalitatem necesse est omnem convenire ecclesiam.*), that is, the faithful everywhere; seeing that in it, ever, by those who are everywhere, the apostolic tradition has been preserved." (Hæres. iii. 3.)

The following are from "Faith of Catholics," by The Rev. James Waterworth.

Tertullian (ob. A. D. 240.) said: "Was any thing hidden from Peter, who was called the *rock* whereon the church was to be built; who obtained the keys of the kingdom of heaven, and the power of loosing and of binding in heaven and on earth." (*Latuit aliquid Petrum, ædificandæ ecclesiæ petram dictum, claves regni cælorum consecutum, et solvendi et alligandi in cælis, et in terris potestatem.—Præscript. n. 22. p. 209.*) He also said: "Remember that the Lord left here the keys thereof (of heaven) to Peter, and through him, to the Church." (*Memento claves ejus hic Dominum Petro, et per eum, ecclesiæ reliquisse.—Scorpiace, n. s. p. 496.*) So spoke Tertullian before he joined the Montanists.

Origen (ob. A. D. 254.) said: "Peter was, by the Lord, called a rock, since to him is said, Thou art Peter, and upon this rock I will build my Church." (*Ipse Petrus a Domino petra est appellatus, cum dicitur ei, Tu es Petrus.*—Comm. in Matt. n. 139, p. 927.)

St. Cyprian (ob. A. D. 258.) said: "There is one baptism, and one Holy Ghost, and one church, founded by Christ our Lord upon Peter, for (or from) an original and principle of unity." (*Una ecclesia a Christo Domino super Petrum origine unitatis et ratione fundata.—Ep. lxx.*) And: ". . the commencement proceeds from unity, and the primacy is given to Peter, . ." (*Exordium ab unitate proficiscitur, et primatus Petro datur.—De Unitate.*)

St. Ephræm of Syria (ob. A. D. 378.) said: "We hail thee, Peter, the tongue of the disciples; the voice of the heralds; the eye of the apostles; the keeper of heaven; the first-born of those that bear the keys."—T. iii. Gr. in SS. Apost. p. 464.

St. Gregory of Nyssa (ob. A. D. 400.) said: "Through Peter he gave to the bishops the key of the heavenly honours."—T. ii. De Castig. p. 314.

St. Basil (ob. A. D. 379.) said: "One also of these mountains was Peter, upon which rock the Lord promised to build his church."—T. i. p. ii. Comm. in Esai. c. ii. n. 66. p. 604.

St. Gregory of Nanzianzum (ob. A. D. 390.) said: ". . one is called a rock, and is entrusted with the foundations of the church; . . ."—T. i. or. xxvi. p. 454.

St. Ambrose (ob. A. D. 397.) said: "It is that same Peter to whom he said, thou art Peter and upon this rock I will build my church. Therefore, where Peter is, there is the church; where the church is, there death is not, but life eternal." (*Ipse est Petrus cui dixit, Tu es Petrus et super hanc petram aedificabo Ecclesiam meam. Ubi ergo Petrus, ibi ecclesia; ubi ecclesia ibi nulla mors, sed vita æterna.—T. 1, In Ps. xl.*) He said too: "They

have not Peter's inheritance, who have not Peter's chair."
(*Non habent Petri hæreditatem, qui Petri sedem non habent.— T. ii. De Pæn.*)

St. Jerome (ob. A. D. 420.) said: "Meanwhile I cry aloud, If any one is united to the chair of Peter, he is mine." (*Ego interim clamito, si quis cathedræ Petri jungitur, meus est.—Ep. xvi. ad Damas. Papam.*) And: "Yet for this reason one is chosen out of the twelve, that a head being appointed, the occasion of schism might be removed." (*Tamen propterea inter duodecim unus eligitur, ut capite constituto, schismatis tollatur occasio.— T. ii. adv. Jovin.*)

St. Augustine (ob, A. D. 430.) said: "If the order of bishops succeeding to each other is to be considered, how much more securely, and really beneficially, do we reckon from Peter himself, to whom, bearing a figure of the church, the Lord says, Upon this rock I will build my church." (*Si enim ordo episcoporum sibi succedentium considerandus est, quanto certius et vere salubriter ab ipso Petro numeramus, cui totius ecclesiæ figuram gerenti Dominus ait. -T. ii. Ep. 53. Generos. col. 180.*) Also: "Who can be ignorant that the most blessed Peter is the first of the apostles." (*Quis enim nesciat primum apostolorum esse beatissimum Petrum?—Tract, lvi. in Joan. Ev.*)

But we are sometimes told that St. Augustine is against the universal interpretation of antiquity, that Christ built the Church on Peter. Rev. R. I. Wilberforce, in "Church Authority," p. 148, says: "Had St. Augustin, for instance, known that our Lord's words were 'Thou art *Cepha* and on this *Cepha* I will build My Church,' he would not have employed the argument which he does in his Retractations. For after stating that he had often applied the passage to the person of Peter, as he had learned to do from a hymn of St. Ambrose, he adds as a second interpretation, which might be given, that 'the Rock was Christ,' 'and so Peter, named from this Rock, would represent the person of the Church, which is founded upon this Rock, and has received the keys of the Kingdom of Heaven.' And then he proceeds, as the reason for giving such an interpretation: 'For it was not said to him, Thou art *Petra*, but Thou art *Petrus*.' Now, of this distinction between the masculine and the feminine word, the original Syriac affords no trace." "In fact St. Augustine," says Palmer, "leaves it to the choice of the reader to understand the 'rock,' either to mean St. Peter or our Lord himself." ('Church,' Vol. II. p. 485.) He then gives St. Augustine's words: "*Harum autem duarum sententiarum, quæ sit probabilior eligat lector.*" So much for St. Augustine's opposition to the sense of antiquity! But no churchman of his time more urgently insisted upon unity with, and deference to, the Chair of St. Peter, than did St. Augustine. In fact, its necessity, as *the* means of preserving the unity of the Church, was his one powerful argument against the Donatists. In the hymn that he composed against them, he said:—

"Come, Brethren, if you wish to be engrafted in the vine;
We grieve to see you lie thus cut off from it,
Number your Bishops from the very chair of Peter,
(Numerate Sacerdotes vel ab ipsa Petri Sede,)
And in that list of Fathers trace the succession,
This is the Rock *(Ipsa est Petra)* against which the proud Gates of hell do not prevail."

And Dr. Ives, in "Trials of a Mind," gives the following testimonies from St. Augustine, which he took from "the before unpublished works of St. Augustine and other Fathers, by that eminent scholar, Cardinal Maius."

"He who would have part with Christ, must be in communion with Peter." *(Communicet Petro qui vult partem habere cum Christo.—T. vi. p. 546., Card. Maius. Ed.)* And: "Do not suppose that you hold to the true Catholic faith, unless you hold that Faith which is preserved at Rome." *(Non crederis veram fidem tenere Catholicæ, quæ fidem non doces esse Servandam Romanam. – Sermon cxx.)*

As the following quotations are given by DuPin, an extreme Gallican, and have been filtered through a Protestant pen, they must surely be authentic and pure:

St. Cyprian. – "After all these irregularities, after having elected an heretic to be a Bishop, they have still the impudence to go to Rome, and carry letters from schismatics to the chair of St. Peter, to that chief church which is the spring of sacerdotal unity."

St. Hilary of Poitiers (ob. A. D. 368.). – "O happy Foundation of the Church, in the change of your name! O Rock, worthy of the building of Jesus Christ, since it was to abrogate the laws of hell, to break its gates, and to open all the prisons of death! O happy porter of heaven, to whom are entrusted the Keys of admission into it, and whose judgment on earth, is a fore-judging of what is done in heaven, since whatsoever he binds or looses upon earth, shall be bound or loosed in heaven."

St. Optatus (ob. circa. A. D. 385.). "For you cannot deny but St. Peter, the chief of the Apostles, established an episcopal chair at Rome; this chair was one, that all others might preserve unity by the union they had with it; so that whosoever set up a chair against it, was a schismatic and an offender."

DuPin says that St. Cyril of Jerusalem (ob. A. D. 386.), in his 11th Lecture, "calls St. Peter the Prince or the Chief of the Apostles, and the Sovereign preacher of the Church." And in his 17th, "He calls St. Peter, the Prince of the Apostles, and the Porter of heaven."

St. John Chrysostom (ob. A. D. 407.). "For it is one of the prerogatives of our city to have had for our master St. Peter, the first of the Apostles. It was just, that that city, which had the advantage of bearing first the name of a Christian city, should have for her bishop the first of the Apostles: but having enjoyed that happiness, we would not ingross it to ourselves, but consented he should go to Rome, the imperial city: yet in giving we have not lost him, we have him still; we have not his body, but his Faith; and having St. Peter's faith, we may truly say, we have St. Peter himself." DuPin says: "S. Chrysostom speaking of S. Peter in that Homily, calleth him the Head of the Body of the Apostles, the Mouth of the Disciples, the Firmament of the Faith, the Foundation of Confession, and the Fisherman of the whole earth."

St. Jerome.—"I am tied to your holiness's communion, that is to St. Peter's chair; I know that the Church is founded upon that Rock. Whosoever eateth the lamb out of that house, is a profane man. Whosoever is not found in that house shall perish by the flood. But forasmuch as being retired into the desert of Syria, I cannot receive the sacrament at your hands, I follow your colleagues the bishops of Egypt: I do not know Vitalis; I do not communicate with Meletius; Paulinus is a stranger to me. He that gathereth not with us, scattereth." (Letter to Pope Damasus.)

Theodoret (ob. A. D. 457.), in his 86th letter, called St. Peter "the Prince and Head of the Apostles;" and, in the 113th, "complimented him (Pope Leo) about his Primacy."

St. Augustine.—"Not to speak of that wisdom and understanding which few men apprehend in this life, several motives keep me in the bosom of the Catholic Church; the general consent of nations and people, an authority grounded upon miracles, upheld by hope, perfected with charity, and confirmed by antiquity; THE SUCCESSION OF BISHOPS FROM ST. PETER TO OUR TIME; and the name of the Catholic Church, which is so peculiar to the true Church, that though all heretics call themselves Catholics, yet when you ask in any country whatsoever, where Catholics meet, they dare not show the place of their assemblies."

Peter Chrysologus (ob. A. D. 460.).—"We exhort you, my most honoured brother, to submit to what hath been written by the bishop of Rome, because S. Peter, who lived and presided in his see, teaches the true faith to those that inquire after it. As for us, we dare not, for the love we have to peace and truth, concern ourselves either to hear or judge causes without the consent of the Bishop of Rome." (Letter to Eutyches.)

In the 4th General Council, "Chalcedon," the Fathers cried in one voice, "Peter has spoken through Leo." (*Petrus per Leonem locutus est.*) In the 6th, they cried, "Peter has spoken by Agatho." (*Per Agathonem Petrus loquebatur.*) Blunt (Key to Ch. Hist., p. 69.) says: "Four General Councils are *officially* acknowledged by the Church of England as binding on her members, and to these are commonly added two (the 5th and 6th), held somewhat later at Constantinople." Why do they not remember, then, the expressions used by the Fathers of these Councils?

For more than these few, promiscuous citations I have not room. In any work on the subject, plenty can be found (classified too) to satisfy any one, not bitterly and blindly biassed against the Church, that, from the works of the early Church writers, an unbroken *catena* of the most express statements can be collected, which show, that from the first the Primacy of St. Peter has been "a fundamental" dogma of the Church. Mr. Palmer says: "I allow that St. Leo and other Roman Pontiffs were occasionally led to magnify the privileges of St. Peter, etc." ('Church,' Vol. II. p. 491.) But how was it, that none of the thousands of bishops who lived remote from Rome, and had no apparent interest in the aggrandizement of the Roman See, did not arise in opposition to the "towering pretensions" of the Popes? No acuter churchmen have ever lived than were those who flourished in the fourth and fifth centuries, at the very time, according to

Messrs. Palmer & Co., when the Popes, publicly and defiantly, imposed upon the Church their oppressive rule. It is a great pity that some of the modern "Catholics" did not live earlier. Had one of them bloomed out in Pope Leo's time, stirred up the bishops to a sense of their common rights, and dispelled the illusion of St. Peter's Primacy, he would have been hailed as a liberator, or have been hissed into obscurity.

If I understand Mr. Palmer aright, there was a time when the Church was free of "Papalism;" there was in early times a non-Papal Church which became Papal. The first was good, very good: the last has been bad, essentially bad. Where was the division? He does not give it. The change could not have been effected without a stormy opposition from some quarter. Like the change from Presbyterianism to Episcopacy, there must be a history of it. By partly re-quoting Mr. Palmer, it can be said: "How improbable is it, that Papalism could have been introduced into all churches, by merely human authority, without exciting opposition in some quarter." The Rev. R. I. Wilberforce's opinion is more consonant to reason, and just as reverent. He says: "Now, if it was a divine power, and not any worldly wisdom, which directed the Christian community in its doctrinal determinations, it must have been the same principle which moulded its Hierarchy, and which fixed the position of its chief."

But, if every thing else fail, the Scriptures are sufficient for St. Peter.

I will finish this letter with an extract from Dr. Stone's "Invitation Heeded," a solid, elegant book. "The Primacy of the See of St. Peter is the most prominent fact in the history of Christianity. And it is a fact which is inseparably associated with a distinct prophecy. Moreover, the Primacy is not only professedly grounded upon the prophecy in question, but is actually so grounded. I do not speak yet of any divine correlation between the prediction and the event, but merely of such connection as is a matter of historical certainty. I mean that the words of Christ are so substantially the foundation of the Papal power that the latter could never have existed without the former. No intelligent student will think of denying this. Indeed, without looking into the past at all, it is perfectly plain that, if it were not for the divine sentences so often quoted, the Pontifical claims would be wholly without sanction, and the Papacy would fall to pieces in an hour. Such being the case, I affirm that the admission of Christ's divinity compels also the admission that the connection between the prediction and the event is of divine intention, and exhibits the most literal illustration of the saying of the Apostle that the Son of God upholdeth all things by the word of His power. The fact must be either the fulfilment of the prophecy or its misinterpretation. But the latter supposition is an absurdity. Facts are never misinterpretations of God's promises. Men may misinterpret a prophecy in their own minds, but God never misinterprets Himself in history. It is no answer to this whatsoever to say that men may be mistaken in supposing that there is any essential relation between the words of our Lord and the fact of the Supremacy; for I have already shown that the association cannot be a mere subjective misapprehension, since it is an objective reality. It would be, indeed, sufficiently incredible that God should have uttered a promise which He eternally foresaw would be misunderstood by the great body of Christians in all ages; but that God should have so ordered events in the development of His Church as to make His own words the very prop and corner-stone of a system which opposes itself to His gracious purposes and perverts the truth which He has revealed, this is inconceivable." This may be worth a second reading.

LETTER XIII.

ANGLICANISM.

All along, in speaking of the Catholic Church, I have, in defiance of the propriety expected by "Catholics," applied the single word *Catholic* to the Church, whose visible head is St. Peter's successor, without qualifying it with *Roman*. This may be called either a pitiable error, or a piece of studied impertinence. Had I carefully looked into facts, I should have recognized, that there is but one Catholic Church, and that this one Catholic Church exists in three segregated and distinctly independent parts,—the "Catholic" (Anglican) Church, the Greek Church, and the Roman Church. The problem may be easy enough, but it is altogether too hard for me. And that three disassociated and unconnected units make one solid unit, is thoroughly understood, I have found out, by none but a small body of modern Anglicans. These men say, that the English Church, as by law established, although independent of, and separated from, every other church, is a branch of the Catholic Church, if not the major and most important branch; that it is really the ancient British Church, which in the 16th century shook itself free of the Roman yoke and superstitions, which Pope Gregory the Great so artfully and impudently imposed upon it; that the "Romish" Church in England is a schismatical body; and that throughout the British Empire the Anglican church is the Catholic Church. In continuation they aver, that, prior to the 6th century, the British Church knew nothing of St. Peter's Primacy; that the superstitious beliefs and practices, that beclouded the pure faith for about nine hundred years, were importations from Rome; that at the beginning of the 16th century the conscience of their church awoke to a sense of its corruptions and its servile submission to Rome, and *reformed itself*; and that it is now, not a Protestant church, but the Catholic Church, standing before the world as a witness to the truth, in all its pristine purity.

I adduce most unexceptionable evidence to show that the earliest churches in the British Islands were established by Roman authority and teaching. Collier (Vol., I. p. 27.) says: "But what progress was made upon the infidels: in what parts the Church was settled, and under whom; what successes or discouragements; what revolutions happened in the ecclesiastical history of this island, from the apostles to king Lucius, is altogether uncertain. Length of time, persecutions, and the ravages of war have, in a manner, sunk the memory of these matters." And on page 28, same volume, he quotes Bede for this: "That in the reign of Marcus Aurelius Antoninus, and his partner in the empire, Lucius Verus, when Eleutherius was bishop of Rome, Lucius, a British king, sent a letter to this prelate, desiring his directions to make him a Christian. The holy bishop immediately complied with this pious request; and thus the Britons, being brought over to Christianity, continued, without warping or disturbance, till the reign of the emperor Dioclesian." On page 29, he gives, from the old book of Llandaff, this extract: "That king Lucius sent Elvanus and Medwinus to Eleutherius, the twelfth bishop of Rome, to desire that he might be made a Christian by his instruction. Upon which, the pope gave God thanks that such a heathen nation were so earnest in their applications for Christianity. And then, by the advice of the priests of the city of Rome, they first baptized these ambassadors, and afterwards instructing them more fully in the principles of the Christian faith, they proceeded to ordain them, making

Elvanus a bishop, and Medwinus a teacher; and they, being thus qualified, returned to king Lucius, who, with the chief of the Britons, was baptized: and then, according to the form of Eleutherius's instructions, the ecclesiastical order was settled, bishops were ordained, and the Christian religion farther propagated among the inhabitants." "This account," says Collier, "carries a great air of truth, and seems to have been the original tradition of the British Church." It seems from this, now, that the British Church did know something of Rome before the time of Gregory the Great. And the very fact that king Lucius sent direct to Rome for Christian instruction, passing through France where Christianity was well known and taught, shows that he regarded the Bishop of Rome as the chief instructor of Christianity. So much for south Britain. "In the year of our Lord 431, Palladius, as Prosper informs us, was consecrated bishop by pope Celestine, and sent *ad Scotos in Christum credentes*, i. e. to the converted Scots in Ireland. This author, in his book, '*Contra Collatorem*,' mentioning the care Celestine had to drive Pelagianism out of Britain, adds, that 'the pope, by sending the Scots a bishop, not only secured a Roman island in its orthodoxy, but likewise brought a barbarous one to Christianity.'" (Collier, Vol. I. p. 117.) On the next page, Collier says: "Upon the death of Palladius, Celestine is said to have sent St. Patrick to succeed him, who is supposed to have been the second archbishop in that island. This St. Patrick was furnished with extraordinary qualifications, to make him big enough for his undertaking. . . . When he came to his charge in Ireland, he was wonderfully successful there, and made, as it were, a thorough conversion of the country." (In the Canons of St. Patrick, which Usher admits to be genuine, appeal in the last resort is commanded to be made to "*sedem Apostolicam . . . ; id est ad Petri Apostoli Cathedram, auctoritatem Romæ urbis habentem.)*

"About the same time (432), the Irish churches were founded by Patrick, who was consecrated bishop by Cœlestinus; and these churches were acknowledged immediately, by all the Christian world, to form part of the Catholic Church." (Palmer's 'Church,' Vol. I. p. 215.) On page 216, Vol. I., he says, "In fine, Scotland received Christianity, and visible churches were founded there by the Irish and Saxon churches."

The British Churches, then, were established in the faith by Roman agency; and it is historically certain, that they acknowledged the Primacy of St. Peter. At the Council of Arles, 314, "the bishops of London, York, and Lincoln, sat as representatives of the British churches," (Palmer's C. I. 215.) and must have concurred with the others "that the feast of Easter should be celebrated on the same Sunday in all the churches of the world." (DuPin) They must have heard at the same time, "that *according to custom* the Bishop of Rome should give notice of the day to the churches." DuPin says, too: "At last, the bishops of this Council wrote to St. Sylvester, Bishop of Rome, as *the chief bishop of the world*, an account of everything that they had ordained, that he might publish these canons throughout the Catholic Church." This is DuPin's abstract, a mild one, no doubt. Dr. Ives, in "Trials of a Mind," quotes Fleury, at length, for the conclusion, and in it there is, "since you (Sylvester) have the greatest part in the government of the Church." And the same is in "the chief bishop of the world;" the chief bishop must wield the chief authority. British bishops were also at the Council of Sardica, A. D. 347, at which the famous decrees were issued, respecting appeals to the Bishop of Rome. In their report to Pope Julius, the bishops of this Council said: "This will seem to be excellent and very suitable, if to the head, that is, to the seat of the Apostle Peter, the priests of the Lord from the several provinces report." (*Hoc enim optimum et valde congruentissimum esse videbitur, si ad caput, id est, ad Petri Apostoli sedem, de singulis quibusque provinciis Domini referant sacerdotes.)* In 423, when Pelagianism was rampant in Britain, Pope Celestine, according to St. Prosper, interfered to suppress it. "At the instance of the deacon Palladius, Pope Celestine sends Germanus, Bishop of Auxerre, in his own stead *(vice sua)*, that he may drive out the heretics and bring the Britons to the Catholic faith." On this subject Archbishop Kenrick remarks: "Those who assert the original independence of the British churches, and their *autocephalous* character, forget their Roman origin, the presence of their prelates in Councils in which the prerogatives of the Holy See were distinctly recognized, and the interposition of Pope Celestine to extirpate the heresy of Pelagius, through his envoy Germanus."

But, when the Saxons invaded southern Britain, what of the Church was not annihilated was driven to the wilds. Milman (L. C.) says: "But all were swept away, the worshipers of the saints, and the followers of the heretics, by the Teutonic conquest." Greene (Hist. Eng.) says: "But in Britain the priesthood and the people had been exterminated together." Still, we are not to suppose the destruction so thorough, that all the Christians fell a prey to the sword. Milman has: "Christianity receded with the conquered Britons into the mountains of Wales, or towards the borders of Scotland, or took refuge among the peaceful and flourishing monasteries of Ireland." Again: "The clergy fled, perhaps fought with their flocks, and neither sought nor found opportunities of amicable intercourse, which might have led to the propagation of their faith." So, for more than a century, the few survivors of the British church were cut off from all intercourse with the centre of unity. Driven from their homes and churches, which had been totally destroyed, and reduced to the condition of scattered fugitives, they would hardly be able to preserve their wonted ecclesiastical status, or to keep vividly in mind all their old rites and customs. But their hatred of the Saxons seems to have been bitter and fixed. Milman says: "Nor was there sufficient charity in the British Christians to enlighten the paganism of their conquerors. They consoled themselves (they are taunted with this sacrifice of Christian zeal to national hatred) for the loss of their territory, by the damnation of their conquerors, which they were not generous enough to attempt to avert ; they would at least have heaven to themselves, undisturbed by the intrusion of the Saxon. *Happily Christianity appeared in an opposite quarter.*" The word "happily" seems, in the circumstances, to be sagaciously used; for by the British the English would never perhaps have been rescued from Paganism. Like the British, the English were to get their Christianity from Rome. And the director of the great work was Gregory the Great—a *monk*, a POPE. The deputed agent was the monk St. Augustine, aided by a train of monks. "Unless," says Milman (II. 180.), "he had been a monk, Augustine would hardly have attempted, or have succeeded in the conversion of Britain." "The missionaries landed in 597," says Greene, "on the very spot where Hengist had landed more than a century before in the Isle of Thanet. . . It is strange that the spot which witnessed the landing of Hengist should be yet better known as the landing-place of Augustine."

The conversion of Ethelbert and his nation soon followed. And right here I must observe, that St. Augustine was a "Romanist." He and his attendants invoked the Saints, prayed for the dead, performed miracles, purified with holy water, made the sign of the cross, and made processions with a "crucifix of silver" and "a picture of the Redeemer borne aloft." Augustine tried hard to obtain the aid of the British in his mission labors; but they met him only to quickly withdraw themselves on the pretence of an affront, ridiculously frivolous, and at the very utmost but three points of difference. They were out of the correct reckoning in keeping Easter; had a peculiar rite of baptism; and used the tonsure of St. John, "by which the front of the head was shaved so as to resemble a crescent, or semi-circle, and the hair allowed to fall down upon the back." On nothing else was a sign of a difference started. Short (Eng. Ch. Hist., p. 9.) says, that Augustine "insisted on three concessions only. That they should keep Easter at the Roman time, should use the forms of that church in baptizing, and preach to the Saxons." But, on the supposition that the British church was the immaculate original of the modern Anglican, the Britons ought to have drawn up a pretty long list of "superstitions," which they positively abhorred; while the Anglicans, to be faithful representatives of the old stock, should agree with them in keeping Easter, in their baptismal ceremony, and especially in the "primitive" tonsorial style. Had the Britons, whom Milman just now called "worshipers of the saints" (II. 176.), differed much from the "Romanists," Augustine would scarcely have sought their aid. It is generally said, that the Britons took umbrage at the arrogant bearing of St. Augustine and so refused to co-operate with him: the more plausible probability is, that their hatred of the Saxons blinded them to their duty, and disposed them to attach importance to differences which in other conditions they would submissively have given up. However this may be, they sulked off, quite indifferent to the conversion of the English; but to say that they, expressly or by inference, objected to St. Augustine in his capacity of Papal envoy is a gratuitous venture. *Not one of them denied the Pope's authority.* As far as can be known, the subject was not mooted. It has been pretended that Dinoot, abbot of Bangor, made a speech that tells to the contrary; but Hardwick ("Middle Ages," p. 9.) says: "It is generally regarded as apocryphal, and exists only in very late MSS."

But, as Augustine's character is sometimes assailed, it may not be amiss to offer what Collier says of him. And I will first produce what this historian says concerning the slaughter of the British monks. "Further, that Augustine died in the year 604, and before the slaughter of the monks of Bangor, the learned Wharton endeavours to put beyond all question. As for Augustine's prediction of this calamity, it does not at all infer he was any way instrumental in it. . . Besides, we are to observe, that the defeat was given the Britons by king Ethelfrid, a pagan prince, whose dominions lay beyond the Humber, and by consequence could be no homager to king Ethelbert. For these reasons, there is no manner of likelihood that Augustine should have any interest or correspondence with him." (I. 181.) On the next page, Collier says: "To speak a word or two of him by way of character. He was a very graceful person, lived suitably to the business of a missionary, and practised great austerities; and if he fell into any inequalities of temper, if he was too warm in his expostulations, or strained his privilege too far upon the Britons, it ought to be charged upon the score of human infirmities, and covered with his greater merit. This is certain; he engaged in a glorious undertaking, broke through danger and discouragement, and was blessed with wonderful success. He converted the kingdom of Kent by the strength of his own conduct and miracles, and that of the East Saxons by his agent and coadjutor Mellitus. The spreading of Christianity thus far among the Saxons was a great step towards the conversion of the rest. Let his memory therefore be mentioned with honour, and let us praise God Almighty for making him so powerful an instrument in the happiness of this island." And the Anglican Short, too, says, in his Hist., p. 16, "The Englishman, who derives his blood from Saxon veins, will be ungrateful if he be not ready to confess the debt which

Christian Europe owes to Rome." He does not say, what would puzzle any one to determine, what debt of gratitude *the Englishman* owes to the British Church. But I must go on.

St. Augustine's mission, which opened with so fair promises, and really brought into the Church vast multitudes, owing to internecine strife, became contracted in its limits. About this time missionaries from Ireland entered the north of England, to propagate the Gospel. And this was Rome working through Ireland. In 664, King Oswi convoked a council at Whitby, at which Colman and Wilfrith, the leaders of the British and the Roman parties respectively, fully discussed their ecclesiastical differences. Greene (p. 64.) says: "The points actually contested were trivial enough. Colman, Aidan's successor at Holy Island, pleaded for the Irish fashion of the tonsure, and for the Irish time of keeping Easter: Wilfrith pleaded for the Roman. The one disputant appealed to the authority of Columba, the other to that of St. Peter. 'You own,' cried the puzzled king at last to Colman, 'that Christ gave to Peter the keys of the kingdom of heaven —has He given such power to Columba?' The Bishop could but answer 'No.' 'Then will I rather obey the porter of heaven,' said Oswi, 'lest when I reach its gates he who has the keys in his keeping turn his back on me, and there be none to open.' The importance of Oswi's judgment was never doubted at Lindisfarne, where Colman, followed by the whole of the Irish-born brethren, and thirty of their English fellows, forsook the see of St. Aidan, and sailed away to Iona." Read the rest to, "It was from such a chaos as this that England was saved by the victory of Rome in the Synod of Whitby."

There have been attempts to make something out of Wilfrith's case, his appeal; but Hallam (M. A. p. 346.) says: "The consecration of Theodore by Pope Vitalian in 668 is a stronger fact, and cannot be got over by those injudicious Protestants who take the bull by the horns."

By 668, when Pope Vitalian sent Theodore into England, the succession from Augustine had vanished. The "Apostolic succession" of the Anglican church, if demonstrable at all, must pass back through Theodore. Anglicans can never touch the British Church by "succession." Read this deliberate statement of England's greatest ecclesiastical historian:—"Those who drew these letters-patent seem not to have been aware that the orders in the Church of England are derived from the Church of Rome; if, therefore, the Church of Rome is an anti-Christian society, her authority is gone, and her privileges forfeited; by consequence, she is in no capacity to convey sacerdotal power in ordinations. From whence the next inference is, that the benefit of the priesthood and the force of holy ministrations must be lost in the English Church." (Collier's Hist., Vol. VIII. p. 101.) Now, it is plain to me, that the Anglican Church, both ethnically and by the claim of order, is a stranger to the British Church : but, if a descent could be made out, the work would plainly show, that the present "Catholic" Church is but a comical parody of its original.

It was from Theodore's time to Henry VIII., that, according to the Homily against "Peril of Idolatry," "not only the unlearned and simple, but the learned and wise : not the people only, but the bishops ; not the sheep only, but also the shepherds themselves, . . (this is second-hand) . . fell both into the pit of damnable idolatry. In the which all the world, as it were drowned, continued until our age, by the space of above eight hundred years. . . So that laity and clergy, learned and unlearned, *all* ages, sects, and degrees of men, women, and children, of whole christendom (pretty well distributed), have been at once drowned in abominable idolatry, of all other vices most detested of God, and most damnable to man, and that by the space of eight hundred years and more." This is plain, vigorous talk, for an object; but it betrays a sublime forgetfulness of the continuous British church. And Mr. Palmer, seemingly conscious that careless people may not perceive its true meaning, has singled it out for a special explanation. He says (as if there were any thing obscure in it): "The meaning is, that *some* persons in every class were guilty of idolatry, which is very certain; but not that the whole Church, literally speaking, fell into damnable idolatry, for if so, it must have entirely failed, which would be contrary to the belief of the Church of England." ('Church,' Vol. I. p. 308.) This, of course, is based on the fact, that "*all* ages, sects, and degrees of men, women, and children," is equivalent to "some persons," just a very few. Mr. Palmer abounds in these clever strokes. The whole Church in England, before the 16th century, whether addicted to idolatry or not, was above all other things "Roman;" and she was not only believed in, and trusted to, by kings, statesmen, warriors, and writers, whom all Englishmen might well honor for laying the foundations of England's greatness, framing her laws, establishing her schools, opening her resources, filling the country with the grandest architectural monuments in the world, and raising to the highest pitch her military prowess among the nations; but the Church was also revered by all within the realm. From "all" one or two enterprising spirits of Wycliffe's type may be excluded. Signs of neither the Church's wish nor of the nation's wish to be free of "Romanism" no where crop out in history.

Now let the substantial facts of the beginning of the "Reformation" be briefly but narrowly noticed. And the facts shall be given in the words of highly respectable historians, approvers of the "Reformation." Henry VIII. had been married to his brother's nominal widow, for more than twenty years, when, fascinated by the salacious charms of Anne Boleyn, he began to gather doubts as to the validity of his marriage. He could ease his conscience and gratify his lust, only by obtaining a divorce. But in those times it was hard for even a king to get a divorce. It could not be had at Rome; and Greene says, "the iniquity of the proposal jarred against the public conscience." (p. 338.) (a 'public conscience' at that time of day!) Cranmer's ingenuity suggested that the judgment of the European universities should be obtained. "But," says Greene (p 343.), "the appeal to the learned opinion of Christendom ended in utter defeat. In France the profuse bribery of the English agents would have failed with the University of Paris but for the interference of Francis himself. As shameless an exercise of Henry's own authority was required to wring an approval of his cause from Oxford and Cambridge. In Germany the very Protestants, in the fervor of their moral revival, were dead against the king. So far as could be seen from Cranmer's test, every learned man in Christendom condemned Henry's cause. It was at the moment when every expedient had been exhausted by Norfolk and his fellow-ministers that Cromwell came again to the front. Despair of other means drove Henry at last to adopt the bold plan from which he had shrunk at Wolsey's fall. The plan was simply that the King should disavow the Papal jurisdiction, declare himself head of the Church within his realm, and obtain a divorce from his own ecclesiastical courts." Collier (IV. 163.) cites this: "That the seals as well of certain universities in Italy and France, were gotten (as it were for a testimony) by the corruption of money with a few light persons, scholars of the same universities; as also the seals of the universities of this realm, were obtained by great travail, sinister working, secret threatenings and entreatings of some men of authority, specially sent at that time thither for the same purposes."

And the Church was overcome in this way: "It was

pretended, that Wolsey's exercise of authority as papal legate contravened a statute of Richard II., and that both himself and the whole body of the clergy, by their submission to him, had incurred the penalties of a præmunire, that is, the forfeiture of their movable estate, besides imprisonment at discretion. . . . The clergy however now felt themselves to be the weaker party. In convocation they implored the king's clemency, and obtained it by paying a large sum of money. In their petition he was styled the protector and supreme head of the Church and clergy of England. Many of that body were staggered at the unexpected introduction of a title that seemed to strike at the supremacy they had always acknowledged in the Roman see." (Hallam's Const. Hist., Vol. I. p. 87.) Greene says: "They (clergy) were told that forgiveness could be bought at no less a price than the payment of a fine amounting to a million of our present money, and the acknowledgment of the King as 'Protector and only supreme Head of the Church and Clergy of England.' To the first demand they at once submitted; against the second they struggled hard, but their appeals to Henry and to Cromwell met only with demands for instant obedience. The words were at last submitted by Warham to the convocation. There was a general silence. 'Whoever is silent seems to consent,' said the Archbishop. 'Then are we all silent,' replied a voice from among the crowd, and the assent was accepted. . . . But Cromwell still kept his hand on the troubled churchmen." (pp. 344-345.) On page 347, he says: "It was only when all possibility of resistance was at an end, when the Church was gagged and its pulpits turned into mere echoes of Henry's will, that Cromwell ventured on his last and crowning change, that of claiming for the Crown the right of dictating at its pleasure the form of faith and doctrine to be held and taught throughout the land." Collier (IV. 174.) has: " But this was not all: there was more than money required of the clergy. The king, perceiving the process of the divorce move slowly at Rome, and the issue look unpromising, projected a relief another way. To this purpose he seems to have formed a design of transferring some part of the Pope's pretensions upon the crown, and setting up an ecclesiastical supremacy. And now, having gotten the clergy entangled in a præmunire, he resolved to seize the juncture, and push the advantage. Thus the regale was required to be acknowledged in uncustomary language; and a new submission of this kind put to the convocation. The author of the 'Antiquitates Britannicæ' informs us, 'That the king refused to pardon the præmunire, unless the clergy submitted to own him their sole and supreme head, next and immediately after Christ. Cranmer and Cromwell were suspected to have suggested this thought to the king. The demand of this new title surprised the clergy extremely; they were somewhat at a stand about the meaning; and were apprehensive dangerous consequences might be drawn from it.'" Hallam (Const. Hist. i. 91.) gives: "The aversion entertained by a large part of the community, and especially of the clerical order, towards the divorce was not perhaps so generally founded upon motives of justice and compassion, as on the obvious tendency which its prosecution latterly manifested to bring about a separation from Rome.... But the common people, especially in remote countries, had been used to an implicit reverence for the Holy See, and had suffered comparatively little by its impositions. They looked up also to their own teachers as guides in faith; and the main body of the clergy were certainly very reluctant to tear themselves, at the pleasure of a disappointed monarch, in the most dangerous crisis of religion, *from the bosom of Catholic unity.*" " By an act of 1534, . . it was made high treason to deny that ecclesiastical supremacy of the crown, which, till about two years before, no one had ever ventured to assert. Bishop Fisher, almost the only inflexibly honest churchman of that age, was beheaded for this denial. Sir Thomas Moore, whose name can ask no epithet, underwent a similar fate. . . . A considerable number of less distinguished persons, chiefly ecclesiastical, were afterwards executed by virtue of this law." (Id. p. 37.) Knight (Hist. Eng., Ch. LIII.) shows too that some rigor was necessary to make this supremacy of the crown palatable to the people. He says: "The prior of the London Charterhouse, John Haughton, after a short imprisonment in 1534, had sworn to the Act of Succession, and so had his brethren. But they were with difficulty brought 'to good conformity.' It was not the policy of the government to let them alone. They were respected by the people of London. They were hospitable and charitable. The new statute of treasons were to be tested upon them. If they yielded and acknowledged the supremacy, their example would reconcile others of lower reputation. If they refused, their punishment would terrify the boldest into submission. They had committed no outward offence. They were to be slaughtered for an opinion. There were two houses connected with the London priory; and their priors came to Cromwell, and with Haughton entreated to be excused answering the questions which they expected to be addressed to them. They were sent to the Tower. They refused to accept the Act of Supremacy when brought before Cromwell and others. They were tried by a jury upon this refusal, of course found guilty, and condemned on the 29th of April. From the Tower to Tyburn was a wearisome and foul road for these poor men to travel on hurdles, in their ecclesiastical robes, on a May morning. It was the first time that clergymen had suffered in England without the previous ceremony of degradation. In that dreary procession through busy streets, and through highways by whose sides pitying and wondering multitudes stood to behold this strange and portentous sight, these earnest men quailed not. In the presence of the executioner they quailed not. To the last they refused to submit to a law of the king and the parliament which they held to be contrary to the superior law of their church. They were not the last of these Carthusians who fell in this conflict. Other monks were hanged and headed. But there were ways of killing, slower but as sure, not unknown to the agents of tyranny." Greene (p. 350.) says: "If he struck at the Church, it was through the Carthusians, the holiest and the most renowned of English churchmen."

From all this it is abundantly manifest, that, because the Pope would not grant Henry the divorce that was condemned by every just man of the time, he broke off all intercourse with the Apostolic See, and, by the meanest trickery and the sternest exercise of brutal tyranny, put the church under his feet, and trod it to a shape to suit himself. *The church had no thought of a reformation:* "the king," as Strype says, "made them (the clergy) buckle to at last." Nor can I discover from any of the above extracts, nor infer from the stern enforcement of coercive statutes, that the people were so suddenly overjoyed at "their liberation from Rome," as men of Mr. Palmer's stamp would have us to believe.

Mr. Palmer says, the papal power "was suppressed, not transferred to the king." However this may be, Henry was more officious and absolute in his church than any Pope had ever been in Christendom. By *Act of Parliament* the king's ecclesiastical power was clearly defined: "Albeit the king's majesty justly and rightfully is, and ought to be, supreme head of the Church of England, and is so recognized by the clergy of this realm in their convocations; yet nevertheless for corroboration and confirmation thereof, and for increase of virtue in Christ's religion within this realm of England, and to express and extirp all errors, heresies, and other enormities and abuses heretofore used in the same : be it enacted, by the authority of this present parliament, that the king our sovereign lord, his heirs and successors, kings of this realm, shall be taken, accepted, and reputed, the only supreme head in earth of the Church of England, called 'Anglicana Ecclesia,' and shall have and enjoy annexed and united to the imperial crown of this realm, as well the title and style thereof, as all honours, dignities, immunities, profits, and commodities to the said dignity of supreme head of the said Church belonging and appertaining. And that our said sovereign lord, his heirs and successors, kings of this realm, shall have full power and authority from time to time, to visit, repress, redress, reform, order, correct, restrain, and amend all such errors, heresies, abuses, contempts, and enormities, whatsoever they be, which by any manner of spiritual authority or jurisdiction ought or may lawfully be reformed, repressed, ordered, redressed, corrected, restrained, or amended, &c." (26 Hen. 8. cap. 1.—given by Collier, IV. 248.) It is hard to see how his power could be further enlarged. Of this Act Knight says: "This is a short statute, but of high significance. There was no power now to stand between the people of England and the exercise of unbridled despotism. The most arbitrary man that had ever wielded the large prerogatives of sovereignty had now united in his own person the temporal and spiritual supremacy. The ecclesiastical authority which had regulated the English Church for eight hundred years was gone. The feudal organization which had held the sovereign in some submission to ancient laws and usages of freedom was gone. The crown had become all in all. The whole system of human intercourse in England was to be subordinated to one supreme head—*king and pope in one*. . . . The higher clergy were terrified into the most abject prostration before this spiritual lord."(Ch. LIII.)

Elizabeth's ecclesiastical authority was, after a repeal of some statutes of Mary and a reviving of some of Henry and Edward, mounted to an equal footing, and as arbitrarily put into practice. "Nothing," says Collier (vi. 214.), "can be more comprehensive than the terms of this clause (a clause attached to the Supremacy bill). The whole compass of Church discipline seems transferred upon the crown. And thus, by the queen's letters-patent, passed in the eighteenth year of her reign, her ecclesiastical commissioners are authorized to visit, reform, correct, as well in places exempt as not exempt, all errors, heresies, schisms, &c. by censures ecclesiastical, deprivation, or otherwise.

"For the better maintenance of this act, the oath of supremacy is annexed. &c.

"As to the penalties for refusing this oath, I shall refer the reader to the statute-book. It is further enacted,

. . . And if the person offending was a clergyman, he was to lose all his preferments. The second offence incurs the penalties of præmunire; and the third is made high treason." On page 251, same volume, Collier says: "On Midsummer-day, this year, the queen signed commissions for a royal visitation all over England. One of them, for the archbishopric and province of York, is directed to Francis, earl of Shrewsbury; Edward, earl of Derby; Thomas, earl of Northumberland; . . . .

"Amongst these fourteen commissioners there is never a clergyman, excepting Sandys, unless Harvey, doctor in law, was in orders, which is somewhat unlikely. Notwithstanding this, any two of them are authorized to visit all cathedrals, collegiate and parochial churches; and all degrees of the clergy, the bishops not excepted. They are empowered *to examine them upon the articles of their belief*, the qualifications of their learning, and their behaviour as to morals: and, in case they find them defective, heterodox, or irregular, they are to proceed against them by imprisonment, and ecclesiastical censures. Further, their commission empowers them to deliver new injunctions, to declare spiritual promotions void, to allow competent pensions to those who quit their livings; to examine letters of orders, to give institution and induction, to convene synods, and receive synodals; and to excommunicate those who refuse to pay: to give licenses to preach to those they judge qualified; to discharge persons committed to prison upon the score of religion: to try the causes of deprivation, and restore such as have been illegally displaced: in short, their commission takes in the whole compass of ecclesiastical jurisdiction, and reaches to every part of the episcopal function, excepting ordination, consecrating of churches, and officiating in divine service. And, which is still more singular, Sandys, the clergyman, is not constituted one of the quorum; but any two of the lay commissioners are authorised to transact all this extraordinary business, and to exert the highest censures of the Church. This, one of our learned historians (Burnet) observes, was more than some people understood, and seemed a great stretch of the queen's supremacy. But the author appears inclined to justify the commission, for he subjoins, 'It was thought that the queen might do that, as well as the late chancellors did it in the ecclesiastical courts;' so that one abuse was the excuse for another. But it is to be feared this plea will not hold; for the imitation of an ill precedent is no sufficient defence: besides, lay-chancellors, though they sometimes judge what crimes deserve excommunication, yet they never pronounce the sentence: that solemn part is always performed by a priest. But these commissioners were not tied to the rules of ecclesiastical courts: their jurisdiction was unconfined and paramount: and therefore, as far as it appears, they might have pronounced the sentence of excommunication, without exceeding the bounds of their deputation. And lastly, the chancellors act in the bishop's name, and by virtue of his commission; of the bishop, I say, who has undoubtedly a right to admit to the communion of the Church, and exclude from it. But these fourteen commissioners managed purely upon the strength of the regale. They had no authority but what they received from the queen, who was without question a lay person, and by consequence could make out no claim to any share of the sacerdotal character, nor produce any warrant from our Saviour for the exercise of the keys." I have produced all this to show that the unqualified authority of the monarch over the Church, first assumed by Henry, was revived in Elizabeth, to be a legacy to her successors. Collier is not satisfied with it. In (VII. 105.) he says: "I observe, secondly, that this learned author (Bancroft) asserts, that Christ committed the care and protection of the Church to the bishops and pastors. But he is not pleased to give any evidence for the revoking this commission; that the pastors should be thus reduced only by baptizing a prince, and receiving him a lay member into their society, is none of the clearest propositions. That the Church should lose her authority by making a prince 'a member of Christ, a child of God, and an inheritor of the kingdom of heaven;' that the Church, by conveying so great a benefit, and administering so glorious a sacrament, should lose her power, and forfeit her charter for government; that the case stands thus, I say, will require more proof than is obvious at first sight, or commonly produced upon this occasion." Some Anglicans, who endeavour to uphold the regale, go on the plea of "antiquity!" I cannot quote Collier from (VII. 89.) onwards, to show the hollowness of the pretence, nor need I, as any manual of early history will show what Collier points out, " That this spiritual society was governed by officers of her own for the three first centuries, is beyond all question... That princes were not to settle controversies of faith, and overrule the decisions of the hierarchy in disputes of this nature, is supposed evident from the first four general councils. Thus the Arian controversy was examined and determined by the council of Nice, and not by Constantine the Great. Macedonius was declared a heretic by the council of Constantinople, and not by the emperor Theodosius: the heterodoxies of Nestorius and Eutyches were anathematized by the councils of Ephesus and Chalcedon: neither did the emperor Theodosius the younger, or Marcion, offer to discuss the doctrine, or interpose in the censure. . . . ."

Most writers understand that the "Reformation" suppressed the Catholic Church in England, and established Anglicanism. Greene (p. 349.) says: "While the great revolution which *struck down* the Church was in progress, England simply held her breath." On page 356, he says: "It was by parliamentary statutes that the Church *was destroyed*, and freedom gagged with new treasons and oaths and questionings." Knight (Ch. LXI.) has: "The English Liturgy, and the constant reading of the Lessons in English, were the corner-stones which held together that Church of England *which the Reformers had built up*." Perhaps, too, Mr. Hallam's head was confused, when he wrote: "It is difficult for us to determine whether the Pope, by conceding to Henry the great object of his solicitude, could in this stage have not only arrested the progress of the *schism*, . . ." (Const. Hist., I. 88.) If there ever has been a schism, a breaking off from Catholic unity, it was when "the British church reformed itself."

It must be very provoking to the " Catholics " to be spoken of as Protestants, and to see their church always dubbed Protestant. Yet both is done by all writers that are without the Anglican communion. Knight says that Elizabeth "and her wise advisers had taken their resolution to abide by *Protestantism*." Hallam has: " Nor could the *Protestant* religion have easily been established by legal methods under Edward and Elizabeth without this previous destruction of the monasteries." (Const. H. 1. 99.) On page 127, he says: "But an historian (Burnet), whose bias was certainly not unfavorable to Protestantism, confesses that all endeavors were too weak to overcome the aversion of the people towards reformation, and even intimates that German troops were sent for from Calais on account of the bigotry with which the bulk of the nation adhered to the old superstition. This is somewhat an humiliating admission, that the *Protestant faith* was imposed upon our ancestors by a foreign army." And on page 257, he has: "And, after the council of Trent had effected such considerable reforms in the *Catholic* discipline, it seemed a sort of reproach to the *Protestant church* of England, that she retained all the dispensations, the exemptions, the pluralities, which had been deemed the peculiar corruptions of the worst times of popery." Greene (p. 408.) has: "The quiet decay of the traditionary Catholicism which formed the religion of *three-fourths* of the people at Elizabeth's accession is shown by the steady diminution in the number of recusants throughout her reign; ... The main cause of the change lay undoubtedly in the gradual dying-out of the *Catholic* priesthood, and the growth of a new *Protestant* clergy who supplied their place." (Macaulay, Hallam's Const. Hist., has the "cause" differently worded: "As soon as Elizabeth ascended the throne, and before the least hostility to her government had been shown by the Catholic population, an act passed prohibiting the celebration of the rites of the Romish Church, on pain of forfeiture for the first offence, of a year's imprisonment for the second, and of perpetual imprisonment for the third.") "During the short reign of Edward VI., it (church of E.) became entirely *Protestant*, and, in point of doctrine, assumed its present form." (Short's Hist. of E. C., p. 593.) On page 199, he says: "At a later period, the sentiments of Calvin undoubtedly affected in a great degree the opinions of individual divines of our church; but the formularies which distinguish us as a Christian community had no reference to the theology of Geneva, and are derived, in a great degree, from the Lutherans." "This Article (VI.)," says Boultbee, "is the fundamental one which stamps the Church of England as essentially PROTESTANT." The double emphasis is his own. Perhaps parson Thwackum, in "Tom Jones," stated his position fairly well when he said: "When I mention religion, I mean the Christian religion; and not only the Christian religion, but the Protestant religion; and not only the Protestant religion, but the Church of England."

Some of the Anglicans, too, preach up the absurdity, that their "continuous British church" has been a constant "witness to the truth." Dr. Ives tears the very bottom out of the pretension. He says: "Waiving, for the time, the question of England's *independent* authority in matters of faith, I was here constrained to ask, at *what period* in the history of that authority are we to trust it as a sufficient guide to eternal life? At a period *before* or *after* the Reformation?—The question is reasonable. For she maintains in the person of her most eminent divines, that she is identically the same Church *now* that she was prior to that memorable event. And, if she was commissioned by Christ and sustained in the work of her commission by Christ's presence, promised to His Church for *all days*, she must have had, *at least*, as good a claim to our confidence *before* the Reformation—while she was yet in communion with the *Catholic Church*,—as she had *after* that event, when she was in a state of separation from all other parts of Christ's body. The question, therefore, was still pressed. At *which* of these periods are we to admit her divine authority to "teach" and direct us? To dictate our faith and exact our submission?

Are we to admit that authority when she taught that the *Pope* is supreme head of the Church? or when she taught that *the king* is? When she taught *seven* sacraments in the Church? or when she taught that there are only *two?* When she held *Transubstantiation,* or when she pronounced it '*repugnant* to the *plain words* of Scripture?' When she held ' the Sacrifice of the Mass for the living and the dead' as a *blessed privilege;* or when she cast it away as 'a blasphemous fable?'"

Whoever gives this subject a careful, dispassionate review must come to the conclusion, that the great Anglicans, who have within the last half-century gone over to the Catholic Church, have simply returned to the faith of their fathers.

LETTER XIV.

TRANSUBSTANTIATION.

On no other point of Christain faith are the Catholic and the Protestant doctrines more pointedly in opposition than they are on the Great Sacrament. The Catholics teach, that in the Holy Eucharist the body, soul, and divinity of our Lord, Jesus Christ, are truly and substantially *present:* the Protestants, for the most part, that His body, soul, and divinity are most certainly *absent.* At Holy Communion the Catholics distribute "the *living* bread which came down from heaven:" the Protestants, common bread. Catholics say, that the elements, before they are consecrated, are simply bread and wine; but that, by their consecration, they become the body and blood of Jesus Christ. And this great change is called *transubstantiation.* It is one of the great mysteries of Christianity, and it has been so bitterly assailed and so grossly misrepresented, that the very mention of the word repels many from even considering it; but one that professes a belief of the Incarnation or of the Holy Trinity, can not consistently reject Transubstantiation, because it may be contrary to his senses or above his reason. As the truths of Christianity are revelations of Almighty God to man, *to be accepted by faith*, and not placed before him, to be tried by his limited knowledge and feeble logic, this great mystery, if it is a revelation, must also be admitted and believed by professing Christians.

The Catholic believes it, because he knows it is and has been the teaching of the Church, in which the Spirit of Truth forever abides; so short and sharp is the proof that suffices for him. But his wonder is, that Protestants, who take the Bible for their creed, do not believe with him.

Abundant testimonies from the great ecclesiastical writers can be produced to show, that the Church has *always* taught the corporeal Presence in the Eucharist. "He (St. Ignatius) affirms, that those heretics neglected the poor and the widows, and separated themselves from the public prayers of the Church, and from the Eucharist, because they did not believe that it was the body of Jesus Christ, which had been nailed to the cross for our sakes, and afterwards rose again from the dead." (DuPin.) "Where he (St. Irenæus) proves the Resurrection of the body against the Valentinians, because it is not credible, that being nourished with the Body and Blood of Jesus Christ, it should remain in corruption." (DuPin.) "Most manifestly signifying by these words, that the former people will cease to offer to God; but that, in every place, a sacrifice, and that a pure one, will be offered to him." (*Manifestissime significans per hæc, quoniam prior quidem populus cessabit offerre Deo; omni autem loco sacrificium offeretur ei, et hoc purum.—St. Iren. Ad. Hæres.*) "He is fed on the richness of the Body of the Lord, the

Eucharist to wit." (*Opimitate Domini corporis vescitur, Eucharistia scilicet. Tertullian. De Pudicitia.*) DuPin says that Tertullian, in the second part of his "Book of Prayer," says: "That the Stationary Days, that is to say, those Days when several of the Faithful continued in Prayer and Fasting till Three a Clock in the Afternoon; we must not abstain from assisting at the ordinary Prayers, as if it was necessary to break our Fast, as soon as we have received the Body of Jesus Christ. 'Your Station,' says he, 'will be more solemn. Receive the Lord's Body, and keep it; and so you shall be Partakers of the *Sacrifice*, and you will perform your Devotion the better.'" "That so we as priests who daily celebrate the sacrifices of God." (*Ut sacerdotes qui sacrificia Dei quotidie celebramus.—St. Cyprian. Ep. liv. ad Cornelium.*) "To give them (the lapsed) the eucharist, that is to profane the holy body of the Lord." (*Eucharistiam dare, id est, sanctum Domini corpus profanare. — Id. Ep. x. Mar. et Con.*) Of the Eighth Book of St. Hilary, on the Trinity, DuPin says: "There is in this book an excellent passage for the real presence of Jesus Christ in the Eucharist, where he says, 'That by this sacrament we truly receive the Flesh and Blood of Jesus Christ, who remains corporeally in us.'" St. Optatus (Bk. VI. ch. I.) asks: "For what is the altar, but the resting place of the Body and Blood of Christ?" (*Quid est enim altare, nisi sedes et corporis et sanguinis Christi?*) From the first of those Lectures of St. Cyril of Jerusalem, which are called Mystagogical, DuPin quotes this: "For as the Bread and Wine of the Eucharist, which are nothing before the Invocation of the most Holy Trinity, but Bread and Wine, become after this Invocation, the Body and Blood of Jesus Christ." From the Fourth Lecture DuPin has translated this: "Wherefore I conjure you, my Brethren, not to consider them any more as common Bread and Wine, since they are the Body and Blood of Jesus Christ according to His word.

For tho' your sense inform you, that 'tis not so, yet Faith should persuade and assure you, that 'tis so. Judge not therefore of this truth by your taste, but let Faith make you believe with an entire certainty, that you have been made worthy to partake of the Body and Blood of Jesus Christ. Let your Soul rejoice in the Lord, being persuaded of it as a thing most certain, that the Bread which appears to our eyes is not Bread, tho' our taste do judge it to be so, but that it is the Body of Jesus Christ, and that the Wine which appears to our eyes is not Wine, tho' our Sense of Taste takes it for Wine, but that it is the Blood of Jesus Christ." "Because the just as well as sinners eat the living body which is upon the altar." (St. Ephræm of Syria.—T. ii. Part. 2, Syr. Comm. in Esai. p. 40.) (What are not otherwise indicated are taken from Waterworth's "Faith of Catholics.") "It is good and very profitable to communicate even daily, and to partake of the holy body and blood of Christ, who clearly says, *He that eateth my flesh and drinketh my blood hath everlasting life.*" (St. Basil.—Ep. xciii. ad Cæsariam.) "Rightly, therefore, do I believe that now also the bread that is sanctified by the Word of God is transmuted into the body of the God-Word." (St. Gregory of Nyssa.—T. iii. Orat. Catech. Magn. c. 37, p. 102-5.) St. Ambrose, in his Book of Mysteries, says: "Afterwards you run to the Heavenly Feast, and see the altar prepared, where you receive a nourishment infinitely exceeding that of *Manna*, a Bread more excellent than that of Angels. 'Tis the Flesh of Jesus Christ, the Body of Life, 'tis the incorruptible *Manna*, 'tis the Truth whereof the *Manna* was only the Figure. Perhaps you will tell me, But I see another thing? How do you assure me, that it is the body of Jesus Christ which I receive? That we must prove. We must show that it is not the body which nature hath form'd, but that which the benediction hath consecrated... A virgin brought forth. This is against the order of nature. The body which we consecrate came forth of a Virgin. Why do you seek for the order of nature in the body of Jesus Christ, since Jesus Christ was born of a Virgin contrary to the order of nature? Jesus Christ had real flesh which was fastened to the cross, and laid in the sepulchre. So the Eucharist is the true sacrament of this Flesh. Jesus Christ himself assures us of it: *This is*, says he, *my body;* before the benediction of these heavenly words it is of another nature, after the consecration it is the Body. So likewise of the blood: before consecration it is call'd by another name, after consecration it is call'd the Blood of Jesus Christ, and ye answer, *Amen*, that's to say, 'Tis true. Let the mind acknowledge inwardly that which the mouth brings forth; let the heart be of that judgment which the words express. The Church exhorts her children to receive these sacraments which contain the Body of Jesus Christ." (DuPin.) "But we, as often as we receive the sacraments, which, by the mystery of the sacred prayer, are transfigured into flesh and blood, show forth the death of the Lord." (*Nos autem quotiescunque sacramenta sumimus, quae per sacrae orationis mysterium in carnem transfigurantur et sanguinem, mortem Domini annuntiamus.* St. Ambrose. T. ii. l. iv. De Fide, c. v. n. 122-24.) "For it is not man that makes the things that lie to open view become Christ's body and blood, but that same Christ that was crucified for us. The priest fulfilling his office, stands pronouncing those words: but the power and the grace is of God. *This is my body*, he says. This word transmutes the things that lie to open view." (St. John Chrysostom. T. ii. Hom. i. de Prodit. Judae, n. 5, 6, p. 451-53.) In the second of his Easter-eve Sermons, Gaudentius of Brescia, made bishop in 387, says: "Whereas in the truth of the New Law, it is the same Lamb dead for all; which being offered in all churches, nourishes under the mystery of bread and wine, those that offer it, giveth life to them that have a lively faith, and sanctifieth by consecration those that consecrate the same. This is the flesh of the Lamb, this is his blood. . . It is the same Lord Creator of all things, who having made bread out of the earth, forms his body of this bread, because he is able, and hath promised it. He who formerly changed water into wine, now changeth wine into his Blood." (DuPin.) "None is richer than he (Exuperius, bishop of Toulouse) who carries the body of the Lord in a box of ozier, His blood in glass." (*Nihil illo ditius, qui corpus Domini canistro vimineo, sanguinem portat in vitro.—St. Jerome. T. i. Ep. cxxv. ad Rusti. n. 20, col. 941.*) In his Epistle to Heliodorus, St. Jerome, speaking of priests, said: "They make the body of Jesus Christ, with their sacred mouth." (*Qui Christi corpus sacro ore conficiunt.*) DuPin gives also this from his letter to Hedibia: "Let us acknowledge, that the bread which our Saviour brake, and gave to his Disciples, is the body of the same Saviour. If then the bread that came down from heaven is the Lord's body, and if the wine which he gave to his Disciples is his blood, let us reject those Jewish fables, and go up with the Lord into that great and high room which is the church; let us receive at his hand the cup, which is the New Covenant. Moses gave us not the true bread, but our Lord Jesus Christ did; he invites us to the feast, and is himself our meat; he eats with us, and we eat him. We drink his blood, we daily tread in the sacrifices, the grapes that are red with his blood." In another place, St. Jerome says, through DuPin: "The fatted calf which is offered, to obtain the salvation of repentance, is the Saviour himself, whose flesh we daily eat, and whose blood we daily drink. The reader, who is one of the faithful, understands as well as I do, what this nourishment is, which filling us with its abundance, makes us put forth outwardly praises and holy thanksgivings. This sacred feast is daily celebrated; the Father receiveth his Son every day, Jesus Christ is continually offered upon the Altars." "He has sanctified His own flesh as food for us forever." (*Sanctificavit in æternum nobis cibum carnem suam. St. Paulinus of Nola. Ep. iii. ad Severum.*) "And because he walked here in the very flesh, and that very flesh he gave us to eat unto salvation —but no one eateth that flesh, unless he hath first adored it—we have found in what way such footstool of the Lord may be adored, and we not only do not sin by adoring, but sin by not adoring." (*Et quia in ipsa carne hic ambulavit, et ipsam carnem nobis manducandam ad salutem dedit; nemo autem illam carnem manducat, nisi prius adoraverit... et non solum non peccemus adorando, sed peccemus non adorando.—St. Augustine. Ps. xcviii.*) "The bread which you see on the altar, after being sanctified by the word of God, is the body of Christ. That chalice, yea rather that which the chalice contains,— after being sanctified by the word of God, is the blood of Christ. By means of these things, it was the will of Christ our Lord to bestow upon us His own body and blood, which He poured forth for us for the remission of sins." (*Panis ille quem videtis in altari, sanctificatus per verbum Dei, corpus est Christi. Calix ille, immo quod habet calix, sanctificatum per verbum Dei, sanguis est Christi. Per ista voluit Dominus Christus commendare corpus et sanguinem suum, quem pro nobis fudit in remissionem peccatorum. St. Aug. Sermon ccxxvii.*)

Further, all the ancient Liturgies proclaim that the *Real Presence* was the uniform belief of the early Church. In the Roman Liturgy, "which is believed to come originally from St. Peter" (Fredet), the priest says: "We beseech thee, O God! to cause that this oblation may be in all things blessed, admitted, ratified, reasonable and acceptable; that it may become for us the body and blood of thy beloved Son, our Lord Jesus Christ." In the Liturgy of Jerusalem, are: "That coming, he (H. S.) may make this bread the life-giving body, . . And may make what is mixed in this chalice, the blood of the New Testament." The Liturgy of St. Mark has: "O Lord, our God! send down upon us, and upon this bread and this chalice, thy Holy Spirit; that he may sanctify and consecrate them, as God Almighty; and may make the bread indeed the body, and the chalice the blood of the New Testament of the very Lord, and God, and Saviour Jesus Christ." In the Liturgy of St. Basil, there are: "O Lord! may thy Holy Spirit come down upon us, and upon these gifts which we have presented, and may he sanctify them, and make this bread the glorious body; and this chalice the precious blood of our Lord Jesus Christ." In the Liturgies of St. Ambrose and St. John Chrysostom, the words are similar. "In a word," says Fredet, "let all the Liturgies, Greek, Arabic, Latin, Gallican, and others, be perused; in all of them will be found prayers addressed to the Almighty, that he would consecrate, by his Holy Spirit, the gifts offered, and make them the body and blood of his Son; which is exactly the Catholic dogma of the real presence and transubstantiation." See also appendix to Mœhler's "Symbolism."

I have surely given extracts numerous enough, and full enough, to show that, during the first five centuries, the Real Presence was the doctrine of the Church. All the great writers are witnesses to the fact; and, if the word *transubstantiation* has not so far been used, the complete change of one substance into another, which transubstantiation expresses, has been clearly illustrated. All, who dilate on the subject, say that the bread and wine are, by the benediction, converted into different substances,—into the body and blood of Christ; and the proper word to express so radical a change is *transubstantiation*. This was the belief of the Church in ancient times, in mediæval times, and is her teaching to-day. And what is more, and should confound those who assert that the real presence was invented in the Middle Ages, Transustantiation is to-day the doctrine of the heretical bodies that broke off from the Church, in the fifth century,—the Nestorians, and the varying parties of the Eutychians; it is also the doctrine of the Greek Church. If the Church changed from something to Transubstantiation, by what influence did she prevail on these off-shoots, her envious opposers, to adopt it? I have not seen any Protestant explanation of the matter. Alzog quotes the view of the famous Lessing as follows: "If it be true, as Zwingle asserts, that the doctrine of *merely external signs* was the primitive and original doctrine of the Church, how was it possible that it should suddenly have given rise to the doctrine of Transubstantiation? Would not this have been a dangerous leap in the dark, such as the human reason never takes, even in its most unaccountable wanderings from the truth? And, in order to avoid taking it, should we not in our own case have approached the doctrine of Transubstantiation by a more consistent, if less direct course? Should we not have gone on from merely external signs to *pregnant signs*, as we will call them for the sake of brevity, or to such as are full of meaning and hidden virtue? And, having assumed this much, we should then have passed from signs to *reality*. The process would then be this: First came the belief in *merely external signs*; next, the belief in *signs possessing a virtue*; and finally, a *substituting for any sign whatever* the *reality or the thing itself*. Now the question arises, how did it come about that the transition was made from the first to the second stage without exciting comment or being the occasion of a controversy, while the transition from the *second* to the *third*, effected, as we are told, by Paschasius, was the occasion of much trouble and quarrelling? This is the more remarkable, since the former would have been more offensive than the latter to the faith and religious feelings of the people. Now, as it is absolutely certain that the first leap in this supposed course of intellectual gymnastics was not the occasion of either protest or controversy, it is but natural to infer that no such course ever took place at all, and that the doctrine of the Church was from the beginning what it is to-day." Mosheim (II. 339.) says : "It had been hitherto the unanimous opinion of the Church, that the body and blood of Christ were administered to those who received the sacrament of the Lord's Supper, and that they were consequently present at that holy institution ; . . ."

What I have put together on this subject fully convinces me, that the great majority of Protestant theologians misrepresent the history of this great doctrine. I see plainly enough, that the Church has, contrary to their assertions, taught the substantial presence, from the very first. Like every other dogma, owing to controversy and heretical cavilling, it may have gradually been more sharply defined and accentuated, but the doctrine itself has always been the same. But what signifies all this? Although it has always been held by the body of Christ, whose spirit is the Holy Ghost, the Spirit of Truth, or the Church against which the gates of hell shall never prevail, the Protestant will naturally turn away from all, to find relief in the New Testament.

It is well remarked by Dr. Fredet, in his " Eucharistic Mystery," that : " Of all the actions and discourses of our Lord, during the time 'he was seen upon earth, and conversed with men,' (Baruch iii. 38.) we find but few unanimously recorded by the four evangelists. His public life, his preaching and his miracles at large, his passion, his death and his resurrection ; these are nearly all the facts that we read alike in the four gospels. His genealogy, his ascension, etc. are mentioned only in two of them ; many other important events are recorded only by one, for instance, the Annunciation, by St. Luke ; the flight into Egypt, together with the circumstances which preceded and followed it, by St. Matthew ; the cure of the blind man of Bethsaida, by St. Mark ; the miracle of Cana in Galilee, the resurrection of Lazarus, and Christ's discourse to his disciples after the last supper, by St. John. It was not, undoubtedly, without a just cause that the Holy Ghost so guided the pen of the sacred writers, as to cause certain words or actions of our Lord to be thus related, sometimes by one only, and sometimes by two or three of the Evangelists. With still greater reason may we believe that there was an especial and a strong motive for inducing them all to mention the same fact, particularly when this fact was not necessarily connected with the other parts of our Saviour's life and passion.

"Let us apply this to the Holy Eucharist. Its institution is expressly recorded by St. Matthew, St. Mark, and St. Luke. St. John, according to his well known intent to omit in his Gospel many things sufficiently mentioned by the other Evangelists, and *vice versa*, to mention many others not spoken of by them, does not describe the institution itself, but relates at full length the solemn promise which Christ had made, two years before, of that admirable and divine blessing. Nor is this all ; St. Paul, who in his epistles, does not commonly refer in an historical manner to any part of our Saviour's life, makes an exception for the Eucharist, and relates the manner, the time and other circumstances in which it had been instituted, declaring at the same time that he had received the doctrine which he taught from our Lord himself ;(see 1 Corinth. xi. 23-25.)"

As the same writer points out, in continuation, this careful relation of the Eucharist must be so often repeated for some good purpose. " It was proper that a mystery which is so much above the dictates of our senses, a mystery to be daily renewed in the Church, and which Christ foresaw would be so violently attacked in the course of ages; should be repeatedly inculcated, not only by the unanimous voice of Tradition, but also by the inspired words of all the Evangelists." The vaguest hint would do for the doctrine as expounded by most of the Protestants.

After the prefatory evidence of His divine power in the multiplication of five loaves, Jesus was followed to Capernaum, by the people. After telling them that their concern was more for the loaves than the miracles, He said, "Labor not for the meat that perisheth, but for that meat which endureth unto everlasting life, which the Son of man shall give unto you." (St. John, VI. 27.) "I am the *living bread* which came down from heaven; if any man eat of this bread, he shall live forever; and THE BREAD THAT I WILL GIVE IS MY FLESH, which I will give for the life of the world." Now, if any expression in the Testament has intelligibility, the emphatic declaration, "*the bread that I will give is my flesh*, might be very well selected as a singularly good specimen: the words are easy and the construction could not be simpler. Look at it for a moment. Will you now say that one of the elements is nothing but common bread? Let the one that persists in so rank an absurdity say what was the precise nature of the gift that Jesus promised. He certainly promised something new; and, as the Jews then had common bread, His promised gift must be something far different. The question, "How can this man give us his flesh to eat?, which is often asked by Protestants, was first propounded by the Jews. What was His reply to those unbelieving Jews? Did He say, "You have misunderstood me," and, as was His constant custom, correct them in their misapprehension? His answer was full and emphatic, "*Verily, verily, I say unto you, Except ye eat the flesh of the Son of man, and drink his blood, ye have no life in you.*" And this is even repeated. "Whoso *eateth my flesh*, and *drinketh my blood*, hath eternal life; and I will raise him up at the last day. For my flesh is meat *indeed*, and my blood is drink *indeed*. He that *eateth my flesh*, and *drinketh my blood*, dwelleth in me, and I in him. .... This is that bread *which came down from heaven;* not as your fathers did eat manna, and are dead: he that eateth of this bread shall live forever." Here the inferiority of manna, which was as good as common bread, to the "*living bread*" is clearly disclosed. But the Jews could not stand this talk: they said, " This is a hard saying; who can hear it ?" Jesus asked them, " Does this offend you ?" He softened nothing. " From that time many of His disciples went back, and walked no more with Him." According to the common Protestant theory, that bread and wine are mere commemorative articles, bread an inanimate substance in no way resembling a "body," a living organism, is not all this gross nonsense ? Is it not positively misleading ? But did He mean the eating of common bread and the drinking of common wine, when He said: " EXCEPT YE EAT THE FLESH OF THE SON OF MAN, AND DRINK HIS BLOOD, YE HAVE NO LIFE IN YOU."? Be candid, now, and say.

When He instituted the Holy Supper, "Jesus took bread, and blessed, and brake it, and gave to them, and said, 'Take, eat: *This is my body. . . This is my blood.*'" Here, the Protestants say, we should read, " This 'represents' my body: this 'represents' my blood." Is it not likely, that, if it should be so read, it would have been so spoken ? Can we not credit Jesus Christ with the simple ability to make Himself exactly intelligible ? It is more than probable that He spoke as He intended to speak, and as He wished to be understood. But "this (bread) 'represents' my body" can not grammatically be sustained. In Latin the text is, according to Beza, "*Hoc est corpus meum.*" Now, to suit Protestants, it should be, " *Hoc (panis)* '*exhibet*' *corpus meum*," a morsel of Latin that would be a disgrace to the " Dark Ages:" for *hoc* is neuter, and *panis* is masculine, and every tyro in Latin knows that a noun and its adjective must agree in gender. The same difficulty is in Greek, and scholars that are competent for it say the difficulty is also in Syro-Chaldaic, the language spoken by Christ. Moreover, if the liberty of displacing words in the Testament by words of our own choosing be once allowed, there will be no end to the practice, nor unanimity in the process. But all Protestants are not so hardy as to correct the language of Jesus Christ. The Lutheran Kurtz ("Sacred History," p. 413.) says: "And, in particular, the words of the institution: 'THIS *is my body*—THIS *is my blood*,' which are the words of a testament and must therefore be understood in a strict and literal sense, contradict Zwingli's view. (the common Protestant one) It is further contradicted by the words of the apostle in 1 Cor. 11 : 27, 29, according to which he who eats and drinks unworthily is guilty of the body and blood of the Lord, and eats and drinks damnation [judgment] to himself, because he does not discern the Lord's body; now in such a case, it is evident that *that* Lord must be present. Besides, this view of the Lord's supper, deprives it entirely of its character as a necessary institution; for such a remembrance of Christ, and such an increase of faith can be produced to the same extent, without the assistance of the Sacrament, by many other means that may be employed."

The objections to the *real presence* are varied and purely rationalistic. The principal one is refuted by Hallam. "This doctrine (Transub.) does not, as vulgarly supposed, contradict the evidence of our senses; since our senses can report nothing as to the unknown being, which the schoolmen denominated substance, and which alone was the subject of this conversion." (Const. Hist. I. p. 120.)

The Protestants have given no evidence that they understand the Eucharist. Luther had a "view" of his own, though of a *real presence;* Zwingle's was a very low one; Calvin's was quite different; Chemnitz's was something apart from all the others; and so on. But the Church is in literal agreement with Scripture: the words of Christ have always been her words, and they always will be.

LETTER XV.

A MISCELLANY.

In this letter, I will look at some of those practices and beliefs of the Church, which are particularly obnoxious to Christians of the perfect " evangelical " type. Most of them are, I think, those "monstrous superstitions," which, during the " Dark Ages," were invented by an ignorant but designing priesthood, and which for so many centuries kept all Christendom in mental and spiritual debasement. *Exactly* what those " monstrous superstitions " are, I have not been able to find out; but some of them may possibly be encountered, if a few Catholic customs and tenets be noticed, that are ridiculed by Protestants.

All Catholics make the Sign of the Cross, and at the same time invoke the blessed Trinity. It is called the *Sign of the Son of Man;* and is a public profession of faith in the Holy Trinity. Who but a Unitarian can object to it? But Catholics, to continue in the practice of Holy Church, from her foundation, must make the Sign of the Cross. Tertullian, at the end of the second century, said: " We often Sign ourselves with the Sign of the Cross; if you demand a law for these practices, taken from the Scripture, we cannot find one there; but we must answer, That 'tis Tradition that has established them, Custom that has authorized them, and Faith that has made them to be observed." (DuPin.) Mosheim (I. p. 211.), speak ing of the second century, says: "The persons that were to be baptized, after they had repeated the *Creed*, confessed and renounced their sins, and particularly the *devil*, and his pompous allurements, were immersed under water, and received into Christ's kingdom by a solemn invocation of *Father, Son,* and *Holy Ghost,* according to the express command of our Blessed Lord. After baptism, they received the *sign of the cross,* were *anointed,* and by *prayers,* and *imposition of hands,* were solemnly commended to the mercy of God, and dedicated to his service;.." "Let us not be ashamed of the Cross of Christ: sign it openly on thy forehead, that the devils, seeing the royal standard, may fly far trembling; make this sign when thou eatest or drinkest, sittest, liest, risest, speakest, walkest, in a word, in every action."—St. Cyril of Jerusalem. Cat. 4, p. 58.—given by Butler. St. John Chrysostom said: "Let us carry about the Cross of Christ as a crown, and let no one blush at the ensign of salvation. By it is every thing in religion done: the cross is employed if a person is regenerated, or fed with the mystical food, or ordained: whatever else is to be done, this ensign of victory is ever present; therefore we have it in our houses, paint it on our walls and windows, make it on our foreheads, and always carry it devoutly in our hearts."—Hom. 54, p. 551.—given by Butler. Collier seems to think that the custom is a primitive one. He has: "Thus Fuller has likewise two arguments, to prove Cromwell no papist. First, he used no 'superstitious crossing of himself.' But if making the sign of the cross be a superstitious usage, as this historian insinuates, then all the Christians in Tertullian's time were tinctured with superstition. But Cromwell desired no prayers for him after his death, therefore he was no papist. But if prayers for the dead imply popery, then not only the primitive Church, but our Reformation was popish too: for during the greatest part of the reign of Edward VI., prayer for the dead was part of our liturgy, as will be further observed afterwards." (v. 73.) The Protestant Blunt, too, (Key to Cat. p. 75.) permits the practice. He says: "The *sign of the Cross* is used at Baptism - marked upon the forehead—to signify that the person baptized, being made a member of Christ, is made partaker of Christ's death, and the benefits derived from it. Also as a solemn token that the person must never be ashamed of Christ crucified, whose 'banner' the Cross is. It is also used on other occasions when anything is blessed or set apart for holy use. We may use the sign of the Cross, when saying our prayers, or when tempted to sin, to remind ourselves of the sufferings and love of Christ, of our union with Him, and of our duties as Christians and bearers of the Cross." By this token the primitive Christians were known: by it are their descendants known to-day.

Catholics are often derided, too, for their abstinence on Friday. It is a practice that they inherit from the first Christians. Hase (p. 67.), speaking of the period (A. D. 100—312.), says: "*Wednesday*, and especially *Friday* (dies stationum, feria quarta et sexta), were consecrated as partial fast-days (till 3 P. M.) in commemoration of his sufferings. . . *Sunday* remained a joyful festival, in which all fasting and worldly business was avoided as much as possible, but the original commandment of the Decalogue respecting the Sabbath was not then applied to that day." Mosheim (I. 126.) has: "It is also probable, that Friday, the day of Christ's crucifixion, was early distinguished by particular honors from the other days of the week."

Who would suppose that the original Christians, those Christians whom all Protestants profess to admire, the Christians that braved the terrors and the tortures of the "ten persecutions," who would suppose that they, in their public services, used lighted candles, and fumed incense? Here is incontestable evidence for the facts. "The oldest name for the chancel was Ara Dei, or *Altare ; oblations* were made there, and 'the unbloody *sacrifice*' offered up, and *frankincense* smoked, and lamps were lighted, even during the persecutions of the Church ; even *votive* donations were suspended in the yet rude and ill-constructed *temples* of Christ." (Waddington's Ch. Hist., p. 183.)

Prayer for the dead is not a mediæval addition to the practice of the Church. Christians have prayed for the dead, from the very first. Their Scriptural reference for it is (II Mach. XII. 46.), "It is therefore a holy and wholesome thought to pray for the dead, that they may be loosed from their sins." Those who deny the canonical worth of the Machabees can not shake its historical authority, as showing the practice of the Jews. And this practice, *which Jesus never condemned*, is still maintained by the Jews. It has also been the practice of the Church ; and she, constantly inhabited by the Spirit of Truth, could not possibly have erred in a matter so important. "Wherefore also does she pray for his soul, and beg for him in the interim refreshment, and in the first resurrection companionship, and offers on the anniversary days of his falling asleep." *(Enimvero et pro anima ejus orat, et refrigerium interim adpostulat ei, et in prima resurrectione consortium, et offert annuis diebus dormitionis ejus.—Tertullian. De Mon., n. x.)* "Suppose her married to a second husband, thou wilt pray for thy husbands, the new one and the old." *(Orabis pro maritis tuis, novo et vetere. Id.)* "Give to his soul the holy mysteries ; with pious affection let us beg rest for his soul. Give the heavenly sacraments ; let us follow the nephew's soul with our oblations."*(Date manibus sancta mysteria, pio requiem ejus poscamus affectu. Date sacramenta cœlestia, animam nepotis nostris oblationibus prosequamur.—St. Ambrose. De Ob. Valentin. n. 56.)* "Supplications for the spirits of the departed are not to be omitted." *(Non sunt prætermittendæ supplicationes pro spiritibus mortuorum.—St.*

Augustine. *De Cura pro mortuis, n. 6.*) On this subject Collier has (v. 284.): "But the argument (Bucer's) seems to proceed stronger the other way: for since prayer for the dead is no where condemned in Scripture, the authority of the Church appears a very good reason to remove scruples, and settle the persuasion of the lawfulness of the thing; which is the meaning of that place in St. Paul's epistle to the Romans. To this purpose, St. Austin tells us, '*Quod universa tenet ecclesia nec conciliis institutum, sed semper retentum est, non nisi authoritate apostolica traditum, rectissime creditur.*' That is, 'Whatever is held by the universal Church, and always observed without being settled by any conciliary decree, is rightly believed an apostolical tradition.' And when we have Bucer, Luther, and Calvin, of one side of the question, and St. Austin and the universal Church on the other, it is no great difficulty to discover the casting of the balance." Waddington (Ch. Hist., p. 182.) says: "The use of prayers and even of offerings for the dead was earlier than the age of Tertullian." Palmer ('Church,' I. 518.) will have it, that, at "the reformation," "the church sanctioned the removal of prayer for the departed faithful from the public service." Blunt (Key to Cat., p. 102.) says: "The Church also prays for the departed in the Prayer in the Burial service: 'That we, with all those that are departed in the true faith of Thy Holy Name, may have our perfect consummation and bliss, both in body and soul, in Thy eternal and everlasting glory.'" He quotes the Prayer of Thanksgiving after Communion to the same effect. In the "Life and Doctrine of Jesus Christ," by Avancini, which is adapted for the use of the Anglican clergy, and published by Rivingtons, there is on page 491, "*da viris veniam et gratiam: da fidelibus defunctis requiem, lucemque sempiternam.*" (give to the living favor and grace: give to the faithful departed rest and light everlasting.): on page 479, is: "*ita ut placide ac benigne suscipias de man-*

ibus meis ad salutem mei et omnium tam vivorum quam defunctorum." (for my salvation and of all others both the living and the dead.) Dr. Smith, a Presbyterian, as quoted in *Contemporary Review,* July 1882, says: "The passages (scriptural) relating to the intermediate state are obscure, but they seem to contain intimations of some truths now missing in our doctrine of eternal punishment. All the analogies of experience would lead us to conclude that the disciplinary processes of life must be continued after death. There is no justification for the doctrine of purgatory(!), but it is Protestant tradition, and not Scripture, which forbids to pray for the dead. There seems to be no reason why we should not do so." It is generally allowed, though, that the existence of a middle state is a strict consequence of praying for the dead. And the dread of being launched into purgatory is no doubt the covert reason why Protestants object so stubbornly against the practice of the Church. But why do they hold religious services at a funeral? The man is dead: his fate is fixed. Where is the Scriptural warrant for the sermon of panegyric that invariably avouches him to be in heaven? As careful practitioners of Protestant eschatology, the first brood of Puritans were more consistent than their present representatives: they took a man off and buried him as they would bury a brute. "The dead are to be buried without any prayers or religious ceremony. However, they (Puritans) had the moderation to allow the use of escutcheons, and such other distinctions, suitable to the condition of the deceased." (Collier, VIII. 284.)

The Invocation of Saints is a Catholic doctrine that Protestants seldom examine temperately or represent fairly. Catholics are reported to be "worshipers of Saints." And so they are, in one sense in which the word may be employed, but not in the sense in which Protestants conceive and report it. According to Webster, the word *worship* may mean "to pay divine honors to," or "to treat with civil reverence." It does not always mean the highest kind of honor (*latria*) that must be given to God alone; but it means also an inferior honor (*dulia*) that may safely and piously be offered to those saints reigning with Christ, who "are as the angels of God in heaven;" and, if they are, their sympathy and concern for us is quite plain, because "there is joy in the presence of the angels of God over one sinner that repenteth." (St. Luke, xv. 10.) Catholics believe, that, since it is advantageous for the Christians on earth to solicit the prayers of one another, much more beneficial must it be to ask the intercessory aid of the Saints in Heaven. Hence, they invoke with confidence the intercession of the Saints; and use towards them expressions of reverence that may be called "worship," in its inferior sense. To the common objection, that the Invocation of Saints practically increases the mediatorship between God and men, a Catholic writer, in a late publication, gives a capital answer. He (Di Bruno) says: "This objection has no real foundation, because JESUS is the only Mediator of *Redemption*, and also *of intercession by His own rights and merits;* whereas the mediation of the Saints is *not* a mediation of Redemption but only a mediation *of intercession and this through the merits of* JESUS CHRIST, *their Divine Saviour and ours.* Hence the Church ends all her prayers with these words, '*Through Jesus Christ our Lord.*'" To save space, instead of giving a list of quotations from the early Fathers (an easy task) to show that the Invocation of Saints has always been a Catholic doctrine, I will give an extract from DuPin, who, in speaking of the Christians of the first three centuries, says: "They prayed for the dead, and made oblations for them, and celebrated the sacrifice of the mass in commemoration of them; the Christians gave one another a kiss of peace; they called one another by the name of brethren, and continually made the sign of the cross. *They prayed* to *Saints and Martyrs*, and solemnized the day of their death with joy, and were persuaded that they interceded with God in behalf of the living." Mr. Palmer (Ch. 1. 518.) has: "In the same manner she (E. Ch.) removed Invocation of Saints, as leading too frequently to superstition, and even to idolatry." Blunt (Key to Ch. Hist., p. 119.) says, that Invocations of "the Blessed Virgin Mary and the Saints" rest on a "justifiable faith in the intercessions of the Saints for the Church on earth, and the wish to obtain a share in their prayers." Quite recently the "Spiritual Combat" has been translated into English. Its *Advertisement* says: "This book forms one of a series of works provided for the use of members of the English Church. The process of adaptation, in the case of this volume, is not left to the reader, but has been undertaken with the view of bringing every expression, as far as possible, into harmony with the Book of Common Prayer and Anglican Divinity." On the 126th page of this book, there is: "The second is: to ask God that those pure and blessed ones may pray and intercede for us, who would not only desire our perfection; but also, if it was the Divine Will that it should be so, that we might attain a far higher position than that which they have: and to beseech Him, that His holy Angels, as 'ministering spirits' may aid us in the midst of our struggles and trials, and especially that they may guard us in our last hour from the powers of darkness." How close this may be to the original I can not say; but, in "the process of adaptation," there has likely been a little circumlocution. Scupoli, probably, like all Catholics, asked the Saints to ask God, and not God to ask the Saints to ask Him; but after all it is several removes from Mr. Palmer's "reformed" position, and he must be grievously shocked to see the tendency to a "superstitious" backsliding of his brethren. On the next page of the same book, this can be seen: "Think often, too, of the Blessed Virgin; *of your guard-*

ian angel; of St. Michael, the Arch-angel; and of any other Saint or Angel, with whom by some circumstance you are especially connected, or for whose spiritual excellence, the Holy Ghost has given to you a great admiration; or whom you are by the secret workings of Divine Grace drawn to imitate." On this subject Collier (v. 393.) has a very sensible paragraph: "Notwithstanding this reasoning, it is certain that angels have part of the administration of our Saviour's kingdom assigned them; and that they are concerned in the presidency and guardianship of the faithful. Thus we are taught by the author to the Hebrews, that 'they are all ministering spirits, sent forth to minister for them who shall be heirs of salvation.' And may it not be part of their employment, to inspect the behaviour, to report the devotions, and intercede in behalf of their charge? If it is said that God Almighty is omnipresent, and needs no information; to this it may be answered, he is omnipotent too, and therefore, has no need of the ministry of angels to assist him in his government, and protect his Church, and yet the Scripture acquaints us he is pleased to make use of them for this last purpose. It is hard for us to pronounce upon the extent of an angel's commission, or to what charitable offices their own benevolence may carry them. It is true, St. Paul mentions 'one mediator between God and man, the man Christ Jesus.' But then, by the next verse it is plain, he means a mediator of redemption, and not a mediator of intercession, so far as to exclude all others. For every one who solicits his neighbour's happiness, and recommends him to God in his devotions, may be said to be a mediator in a lower sense. Now such instances of charity are not only lawful; but the duty of one Christian towards another. And that an angel is barred the liberty of such friendly applications, is more than Bucer has proved." "It is a sublime and beautiful doctrine, inculcated by the early fathers, that there are guardian angels appointed to watch over cities and nations; to take care of the welfare of good men, and to guard and guide the steps of helpless infancy." (Washington Irving's St. Mark's Eve, in Bracebridge Hall.)

Many people consider "confession to a priest" as a very humiliating and unnecessary ordeal, and the "priestly absolution" that follows it, a scandalous assumption of divine power by a man. Are we not told, though, in the Testament, to confess our sins? And, as it stands, it is a positive command, subject to no conditions of taste or fancy. "And were baptized of him in Jordan, confessing their sins." (St. Matt. III. 6.) "And many that believed came, and confessed, and showed their deeds." (Acts, XIX. 18.) "Confess your faults one to another." (Jas. v. 16.) From these texts it is quite manifest, that a confession is a recital of specific transgressions, and not a statement made by a penitent, in a general way, that he is a sinner, just as a saint might put it. To come up to the tenor of the texts, a full confession of particular sins must be made. But to whom must it be made? To a "physician of souls?" or to a party having neither authority to pronounce on the matter, nor even knowledge to give advice? In the Church it has always been made privately to a priest. And this confession to a priest is a particular degradation, as contrasted with a confession before an assembly of "saints" and sinners! Were it a matter purely of choice, I would greatly prefer to disclose my secrets to one, who would part with his head before he would betray to any one else a syllable, than to a crowd of scandalmongers who would magnify every peccadillo and gloat over my acknowledged frailties, for weeks afterwards. If there be any thing degrading in a confession, it will be seen, if carefully looked into, that the Church, by enforcing "auricular confession," has it in a form as agreeable and safe as possible. Confession to a *priest* has always been the practice of the Church. "In his (Origen's) time (185 –254.) sins were confessed to the priests." (Du Pin.) Mosheim (1. 130.), speaking of the first century, says: "Those who were visited with violent, or dangerous disorders, sent, according to the apostle's direction (Jas. v. 14.), for the rulers of the church, and, after confessing their sins, were recommended by them to the divine mercy, in prayers full of piety and fervour, and were also anointed with oil." Collier (v. 253.) has: "Now since private confession was thus customary in the ancient Church, since there was a person particularly appointed for this purpose, we must conclude it was then thought a very serviceable expedient." "The practice of private confession to priests, and absolution, she (E. Ch.) never abolished." (Palmer's Ch. 1. 518.) Short, Hist. of Ch. of Eng., p. 170, says, that "reason, as well as the word of God, strongly points out, that to acknowledge our faults, especially to one vested with spiritual authority over us, must be a most effectual means of restraining us from the commission of sin. . . In the Church of England the confession of particular sins is recommended in the Exhortation to the Sacrament, and the Visitation of the Sick: but so little are we accustomed to this most scriptural duty, that these recommendations are frequently unknown and generally neglected." For the power of absolution, this should be sufficient: "*As My Father hath sent Me, even so send I you.* And when He had said this, He breathed on them, and said unto them, Receive ye the Holy Ghost: *Whosesoever sins ye remit, they are remitted unto them; and whosesoever sins ye retain, they are retained.*" (St. John, xx. 21-23.) Read also St. Matt. xviii. 18. If now we turn to St. Matt. ix. 6, we can see that Jesus, as *the Son of man*, forgave sins, and that the multitude "glorified God, *which had given such power unto men.*" Jesus, *as the Son of man*, forgave sins; and this power which He received of the Father, He transferred to His Apostles, when He said, "As my Father hath sent Me, even so send I you." St. Paul exercised this power: in 11 Cor. II. 10, he says, "For your sakes forgave I it *in the person* of Christ." And the same power resides in every lineal descendant of the Apostles. A priest forgives sins, not as a mere man, but as a minister of Christ, and, as he acts by His commission, so he forgives sins in His name. By what ingenious quirk the above text from (St. John, xx.) can be contorted to a meaning at variance with its clear, literal significance, I can not discover. All the " evangelical " commentators, whose works I have consulted, either skip over it as if it were something to be piously ignored, or give it an explication that reduces it to an absurdity.

Whoever confesses a belief in post-apostolic miracles advertises at once his grovelling credulity. The miracles of the Old Testament and those of the New may, with certain qualifications, merit our credence; but after the death of the Apostles, or shortly after, God Almighty suddenly ceased to be Himself. From the Creation to the advent of Christ, He had directly, and through His servants, displayed to the world His omnipotence, in many ways and on various occasions; and during the Apostolic age many of those who believed in Him wrought miracles in His name; but without any warning, without the slightest intimation, He ceased to interest Himself in the affairs of mankind, and no special tokens of His approbation or displeasure have throughout the Christian period been signalized! Where is the philosophy or the Scripture for so ridiculous an opinion? Were the words of Christ, "And these signs shall follow them that believe; In my name shall they cast out devils; they shall speak with new tongues; They shall take up serpents; and if they drink any deadly thing, it shall not hurt them; they shall lay hands on the sick, and they shall recover." (St. Mark, XVI.), or (1 Cor. XII. 8-10.), haphazard promises that have in no instance received a fulfilment? No sane Christian will say so. And it is historically certain, that, since the time of Christ, the ordinary course of events have been repeatedly altered, and the operation of natural laws have been checked, by supernatural agency. Julian, the Apostate, to disprove the divinity of the Christian religion, undertook to re-build the temple of Jerusalem, but wofully failed. Both Pagan and Christian writers of the time give unanimous testimony to the fact. Mosheim (I. 332.) says: "All, however, who consider the matter with attention and impartiality, will perceive the strongest reasons for embracing the opinion of those who attribute this event to the almighty interposition of the Supreme Being; nor do the arguments offered by some, to prove it the effect of natural causes, or those alleged by others to persuade us that it was the result of artifice and imposture, contain any thing that may not be refuted with the utmost facility." Hase (Ch. Hist., p. 64.) says: "He (St. Anthony— ob. A. D. 356.) was without human learning, but endowed with eminent natural abilities, and in the service of the King of kings was exalted above the fear, as he was afterwards above the favor of earthly monarchs. His word healed the sick and cast out devils. When his prayers were answered, as they not unfrequently were, he boasted not of his power, nor did he murmur when they were unheard, but in both cases he gave praise to God. No angry person went from his presence unreconciled with his adversary, and no mourner uncomforted. He seemed to have been provided by God to be a physician in bodily and spiritual things for the whole land of Egypt." On page 296, Hase says of St. Francis (Assisi): ".. and yet we are compelled to believe that this seraphic stranger upon earth really experienced many things out of the ordinary course of nature." Take another from Gibbon: "Yet the historian, who views this religious conflict with an impartial eye, may condescend to mention one preternatural event, which will edify the devout, and surprise the incredulous. Tipasa, a maritime colony of Mauritania, sixteen miles to the east of Cæsarea, had been distinguished, in every age, by the orthodox zeal of its inhabitants. They had braved the fury of the Donatists; they resisted, or eluded, the tyranny of the Arians. The town was deserted on the approach of an heretical bishop: most of the inhabitants who could procure ships passed over to the coast of Spain; and the unhappy remnant, refusing all communion with the usurper, still presumed to hold their pious, but illegal, assemblies. Their disobedience exasperated the cruelty of Hunneric. A military count was despatched from Carthage to Tipasa: he collected the Catholics in the Forum, and, in the presence of the whole province, deprived the guilty of their right hands and their tongues. But the holy confessors continued to speak without tongues: and this miracle is attested by Victor, an African bishop, who published a history of the persecution within two years after the event..... They (other witnesses) all lived within the compass of a century; and they all appeal to their personal knowledge, or the public notoriety, for the truth of a miracle, which was repeated in several instances, displayed on the greatest theatre of the world, and submitted, during a series of years, to the calm examination of the senses." (Hist., III. 557.) "As for St. Alban's miracles, being attested by authors of such antiquity and credit, I do not see why they should be questioned. That miracles were wrought in the Church, at this time of day, is clear from the writings of the ancients. To suppose there are no miracles but those in the Bible, is to believe too little. To imagine that God should exert his omnipotence, and appear supernaturally for his servants in no place but Jewry, and in no age since the Apostles, is an unreasonable fancy: for since the world was not all converted in the apostles' times, and God designed the further enlargement of His Church, why should we not believe He should give the pagans the highest proof of the truth of Christianity, and honour his servants with the most undisputed credentials? Now if this is very reasonable to suppose, why should St. Alban's miracles be disbelieved, the occasion being great enough for such an extraordinary interposition? For, by this means, the martyr must be mightily supported, the British Christians fortified against the persecution, and the pagans surprised into a conversion." (Collier, I. 52.) Baring-Gould, in preface of " Lives of Saints," speaking of mediæval times, says: " The evidence for miraculous cures by living Saints, or by their relics is overwhelming." Palmer (Ch. I. 145.) provides this: " Far it be from me to affirm that real miracles have not been wrought since the time of the apostles, for the confirmation of Christians, and especially for the conversion of the heathen. There is every probability, nay certainty, that such signs have been wrought; . ." And the Calvinist Shedd, in his " History of Doctrine," (I. 166.), quotes the Protestant Quenstedt as admitting, that the Jesuits have performed miracles in India and Japan. Quenstedt's words are : " *Nolim negare Jesuitas in India et Japonica vera quædam miracula edidisse.*" But the Methodist Watson will tolerate nothing of the kind after the apostolic age: I wonder whether he ever terrified an audience with a story about some "Sabbath" breaker that was visited by the hand of God?

Have I ever heard or noticed, that a priest in a church speaks in an "unknown tongue?" I have certainly heard something about it, and I know that the Ordinary of the Mass is recited in Latin, though in the Prayer Book every column of Latin has a parallel column in English, making the Office perfectly intelligible to every one that can read at all. But the Protestant that neither understands Latin, nor can conceive any excuse for its use by the Church, feeling his utter helplessness in its presence, and compassionating, in the exuberance of his charity, the condition of those Catholics that are no better qualified for it than himself, cries piteously for its total disuse. Latin is to him an "unknown tongue." This is astonishing. How is it that a single Protestant can be found, who is ignorant of Latin, which has been for centuries upon centuries the language of scholars and the schools? One would think that the "glorious reformation," that great disseminator of learning, would by this time have so managed matters as to make the most important of the classics the property of the multitude. In times gone by, every boy that had any knowledge of letters whatever had Latin all right: he had Latin and his mother tongue. To be sure, from the superstitious tastes of his teachers, he may have been tied down to indifferent models of the language; instead of being allowed to gloat over the fascinating pages of Ovid or Martial, he may have been forced to content himself with extracts from S. Severus, or S. Optatus, or S. Augustine, or Lactantius, or even Salvian; but, however imperfect his course of reading may have been, he would not detect any "unknown tongue" in the Office of the Mass. After the suppression of the monasteries, only a few privileged ones could acquire a knowledge of Latin: the agencies, encouraged by the Church for its general diffusion, have been overthrown, and now it has to be called an "unknown tongue." Yet its acquisition is possible to-day, and the little necessary to understand what is in the Catholic worship can be acquired readily and easily. The only obstacle is laziness or indifference. But why did the Church adopt an "unknown tongue?" She never did so. When she made Latin her own, Latin was the language of the world. It was the language of the Romans, who conquered the world. It was then the universal language, and what other language could be used by the universal Church? But, allowing that the Latin was the only language she could use for more than a thousand years, why does she cling so affectionately to it now? The reasons, if fully given, would fill a volume: because, as every one who gives the subject any thought will see that the one Church spread over the earth must have one language, she has every reason to hold to the Latin which has been the indirect instrument of all her victories; because in it are embodied all her history, her laws, the papal utterances, her theology, and every kind of record worthy of preservation; and because, as the Latin in its flexions and idioms is fixed, it is an unchangeable language and consequently the most appropriate for an unchangeable Church. The Church, then, will continue to keep her own language. But why does she celebrate the mass in Latin? Because, as the Mass is a sacrifice and must necessarily be offered by a priest, and as it can not signify any thing to the congregation in what language he recites the sacramental words of intercession, which are always too low for the people to hear, there can be no reason why the very words should not be constantly and universally used, that have been constantly and universally used, nor why the priest should not use the words for which he must have a reverential preference. And what can be sublimer than one office conducted throughout the world, in one exact form of words? It matters not where a Catholic goes he everywhere finds the Mass the same; and he everywhere understands it, and can join in the worship. This difficulty of an "unknown tongue" will not disturb his religious convictions. He knows that in the "meeting house" there are singing, preaching, and praying, in English: but he knows also that in a Catholic church there are singing, preaching, and praying, in English, and one GOOD EXTRA in the language of the Church.

Now that I have shown the principal reasons that prevailed with me in adopting Catholicity, I can not fairly be accused of having acted on a sudden impulse, or by a fanciful freak. So far was my action from any thing of the kind, that I had fully made up my mind to be a Catholic for more than a year before I offered myself for baptism. At midsummer of 1886, I was duly instructed and prepared by the Rev. Father Allain, then parish priest of Uxbridge, Ont., who baptized me and received me into the Church. And, as I have been a Catholic for more than two years, and have consequently well tided over the probationary period of six months, which is usually allowed for giddy-headed converts to tire of the "tinsel trumperies" of Catholicity, I now consider myself irrevocably established in the faith of my fore-fathers. A Catholic I am proud to declare myself; a Catholic I intend to be; and in the Catholic Church I hope to die.

INDEX.

Absolution 207. **Albert the Great** 30. **Anglicanism** 160, is Prot. 181, orders from Rome? 169. **Augustine, St.** 167.

Benedictines 40. **Bible before Luther** 55. **British Churchmen monks** 41

Calvin 86. **Carthusian martyrs in England** 174. **Church** 107, visible 110 119, one 113 121, holy 114 121, catholic 114 123, apostolical 115 124, infallible 116 126, advocate of popular rights 66 67, church architecture originate with monks 44. **Commandments** 58. **Confession** 206. **Cranmer** 88

"**Dark Ages**," not times of ignorance 30. "**Decretals**" 74. **Dinoot's Speech** 166.

Edict of Milan 71. **Edwards's Lamentation** 94. **Elizabeth** 91. **English clergy opposed to reform** 172. **Epistles not in Canon** 134.

Friday 199.

Greek well known in Middle Ages 29. **Guardian Angel** 201.

Hear the Church 128. **Henry the first "Reformer" in Eng** 170. **Huguenots in France, lawless** 98.

Incense 199. **Invocation of Saints** 202.

Jesuits maligned 49, in Brazil 51.

Kepler persecuted by Lutherans 21. **Knox** 87.

Learning before Luther's time 27. **Luther** 83, dispensation for bigamy 85.

Miracles 208 **Monasticism** 36. **Monks the best missioners** 41 165. **Mosheim corrupts history to combat the Church** 59.

Names of Puritans' children 96

Orange cruelties in Ireland 25 **Orders, three** 139.

Papal Power, origin of 73 **Patrick, St., success in Ireland** 162 **Penal laws in Ireland** 24 **Peter, St in Rome** 147 **Petram** 153. **Polity of Syn. transferred to Ch** 112 **Pope not Antichrist** 61. **Popes, unbroken succession of** 63, successors of St. Peter 148, promoters of learning 29 31 32. **Prayer for dead** 200 **Presbyterianism** 63, in England 93 **Primacy of St. Peter** 138 **Prot ordination "only a ceremony"** 125

Regale 175 "**Reformers" in Mary's reign** 66. **Rule of Faith** 130.

Salvation only in Church 127. **Saying of Middle Ages** 67. **Schools in Middle Ages** 29 43 **Sign of Cross** 197. **Slavery restrained by Church** 67. **Syro-Chaldaic** 115.

Temporal Power 68. **Transubstantiation** 183. **Truce of God** 67.

"**Unknown Tongue**" 211.

www.ingramcontent.com/pod-product-compliance
Lightning Source LLC
Chambersburg PA
CBHW020824230426
43666CB00007B/1093